'The day Dr Amitta Shah walked into our home to assess our son, our lives changed immediately. Her compassionate manner and decades of expertise shone through and I suddenly had an answer to a very big question! I had read about autism catatonia and was sure our son did have it, so when she confirmed the diagnosis, I felt a sense of relief. We had always suspected that his "idiosyncrasies" were more than just traits of his Asperger's or OCD, as we'd been told for years. Through Amitta I learnt everything I needed to know and was able to look back on his life and finally piece together particular events and certain situations. I finally had an explanation as to why he reacted in certain ways and although I knew the road ahead was not going to be easy, with Amitta's help and guidance, we had support and a plan for the first time. I am sure that with this much-needed book, she will continue to help many others, and I for one, cannot thank her enough for the help she has given us as a family.'

*– Nicola Martin, parent*

*of related interest*

**A Guide to Mental Health Issues in Girls and Young Women on the Autism Spectrum**
Diagnosis, Intervention and Family Support
*Dr Judy Eaton*
ISBN 978 1 78592 092 9
eISBN 978 1 78450 355 0

**OCD and Autism**
A Clinician's Guide to Adapting CBT
*Ailsa Russell, Amita Jassi and Kate Johnston*
*Illustrated by David Russell*
ISBN 978 1 78592 379 1
eISBN 978 1 78450 728 2

**Understanding and Treating Self-Injurious Behavior in Autism**
A Multi-Disciplinary Perspective
*Edited by Stephen M. Edelson and Jane Botsford Johnson*
*Foreword by Temple Grandin*
ISBN 978 1 84905 741 7
eISBN 978 1 78450 189 1

**Sensory Perceptual Issues in Autism and Asperger Syndrome, Second Edition**
Different Sensory Experiences – Different Perceptual Worlds
*Olga Bogdashina*
*Foreword by Manuel F. Casanova*
ISBN 978 1 84905 673 1
eISBN 978 1 78450 179 2

**Autism and Enablement**
Occupational Therapy Approaches to Promote Independence for Adults with Autism
*Matt Bushell, Sandra Gasson and Ute Vann*
ISBN 978 1 78592 087 5
eISBN 978 1 78450 348 2

# Catatonia, Shutdown and Breakdown in Autism

## A Psycho-Ecological Approach

## Dr Amitta Shah

Foreword by Dr Judith Gould

Jessica Kingsley *Publishers*
London and Philadelphia

First published in 2019
by Jessica Kingsley Publishers
73 Collier Street
London N1 9BE, UK
and
400 Market Street, Suite 400
Philadelphia, PA 19106, USA

*www.jkp.com*

**Library of Congress Cataloging in Publication Data**
A CIP catalog record for this book is available from the Library of Congress

**British Library Cataloguing in Publication Data**
A CIP catalogue record for this book is available from the British Library

ISBN 978 1 78592 249 7
eISBN 978 1 78450 531 8

Printed and bound in Great Britain

*In memory of my sister, Sheela*
*And my parents, Jayaben and Liladharbhai*
*I have missed them during this journey…*
*And have drawn on their strength, courage and blessings*
*…to persevere and stay on my path*

# Contents

# Foreword

This book has to be the most needed and timely publication and gives a detailed and coherent account as to how to recognise catatonia and to help and support those with this condition.

There is still a false belief that catatonia is exclusively associated with untreated schizophrenia, which can have devastating consequences for the person who has this condition. Dr Shah, together with Dr Lorna Wing, recognised the misconception linking catatonia exclusively with schizophrenia. Through careful deduction and inspirational thinking, they began to widen the concept of catatonia, linking the behaviour pattern with those diagnosed as being on the autism spectrum. This was a major step forward in an understanding of this complex condition. They saw many autistic individuals with different manifestations of behaviour at different levels of catatonia, which are clearly described in the book.

They adopted the dimensional approach to understanding the condition, which is far more meaningful in describing the individual's strengths and difficulties. They stressed the importance of carrying out detailed developmental histories, taking into account all aspects of the individual's life in different settings and at different times. They realised, as in autism, that a holistic approach has to be the way forward in assessing a person to make appropriate recommendations. The old concept of making a medical diagnosis based on counting symptoms suggested by the International Diagnostic Classification Systems is a categorical approach, which is not in any way the best solution to understanding and helping the person concerned.

Dr Shah's enthusiasm and dedication to this client group resulted in her carrying on the work initiated by herself and Dr Wing. Each chapter in the book not only gives theoretical information, but more importantly gives numerous case studies, which bring alive examples of how the condition affects the lives of the person and their family. The dedication of parents in their pursuit to understand their child's symptoms, often at great odds with the lack of understanding of professionals, is truly humbling. Particularly poignant are the case studies of those who have insight into their condition and can describe their reactions and feelings, with high levels of anxiety, when a catatonic breakdown occurs. In reading the case studies, it is understandable why Dr Shah has made this her life's work.

The chapter on misinterpretation and misdiagnosis of the condition shows how a lack of understanding has far-reaching consequences and can lead to very inappropriate treatment. The medical/psychiatric approach alone, without considering the psycho-ecological approach, has historically resulted in very inappropriate management. It is pointed out that acute, severe catatonia can be triggered by the side effects of certain medications. Several examples of case studies are given when this has occurred. Psychiatric medication has often too readily been given. Hopefully, the information in this book will make medical practitioners think carefully before prescribing medication for long-term use without appropriate reviews. Medication may be of benefit for short-term intervention, but using the psychological and psycho-ecological strategies should be employed for long-term support. This approach in supporting those with catatonia makes more sense, since catatonia is clearly not a single manifestation of behaviour. It is a complex, heterogeneous condition with many types of manifestations with a wide range of severity, along several dimensions with huge individual variation. Therefore, the treatment and management needs to be based on a multi-dimensional approach.

Dr Shah's approach is a non-medical, psychological, holistic one. She has developed a framework which covers all aspects of the person's life. Assessing the environment is crucial to understanding the catatonic breakdown, which is often related to high levels of stress and anxiety, together with other external triggers. Once these are evaluated and recognised, a programme can be put in place to address the problems. Examples are given of early indicators which can be the key to prevent a chronic condition arising. By giving detailed examples of different behaviours, it is shown that day-to-day fluctuations can lead to people thinking the behaviours are under the person's control.

This is far from the truth and is often dismissed as they 'can' do but 'won't' do. This has led to many inappropriate methods of intervention.

The treatment approach has to be individually based as the catatonic type breakdown is variable and although there are common factors, the way the disorder manifests itself can be very idiosyncratic and, on occasions, not understandable.

Dr Shah has produced guidelines in the form of the Autism Catatonia Evaluation (ACE-S), which will be an invaluable resource for all professionals. It systematically assesses and evaluates the presence of particular aspects and manifestations of catatonia, shutdown and breakdown. The results of this evaluation, together with observations of the person in different settings, will provide a meaningful way forward. It will help those who in the past have not only been neglected in understanding their needs, but have been subjected to inappropriate treatments.

I highly recommend this book for all professionals working in the field of autism, not only to alert them to the link between autism and catatonia, but in giving practical guidelines on the management and treatment of this fascinating, yet devastating condition.

There are still many questions unanswered as to the nature, causation and neuropathology of catatonia and it is hoped that this book will encourage professionals to carry out further research in this very much neglected field.

Dr Judith Gould
Consultant clinical psychologist,
the NAS Lorna Wing Centre for Autism

# Acknowledgements

So many people have contributed to this project by providing inspiration, ideas and intellectual, practical and moral support. I will not be able to name them all but would like to especially acknowledge and say a very big thank you to the following people:

- First and foremost, I want to make a special acknowledgment to my husband Smit. His relentless and multi-dimensional support and encouragement at every stage has been crucial and invaluable to me.

- Family and friends who have followed the progress and provided inspiration and encouragement at key times. There are too many of them to mention by name. Special thanks to Sohini for her professional input and ideas, and to Apurva, Reyan, Anay and Bindi for keeping me going in their own special ways.

- All the autistic individuals and their families with whom I have been professionally involved over the years: they have taught me so much, not only about autism and catatonia but also about life, endurance and humility.

- All the individuals and parents/guardians who have willingly and enthusiastically given me permission to write their stories in the context of this book.

- Parents, practitioners, therapists, carers, teachers and care staff who have shared strategies and given feedback about implementation of the various components of the psycho-ecological approach.

- Dr Lorna Wing for introducing me to the complexities of the autism spectrum and the concept of catatonia in autism; Lorna has not only been a close collaborator in clinical and research work relevant to this book, but she has been an inspirational mentor, colleague and friend.

- Professor Uta Frith for inspiring me to be interested in all the enigmatic and unusual aspects of autism; her enthusiasm, encouragement and ideas and comments on earlier drafts have been invaluable.

- Dr Judith Gould for her continual professional advice, guidance and support over the years and especially during the course of writing this book; Judith's comments and suggestions on earlier drafts of the book have been invaluable and I am so pleased that she has written the foreword.

- Dr Dinah Murray for reading and commenting on an earlier draft of the book and her encouragement.

- Dr Sarah Lister-Brook for commenting on the ACE-S from a clinician's viewpoint.

- The National Autistic Society (NAS), who have been very supportive as an organisation, and I am grateful to them for giving me a platform at conferences, training events and masterclasses to present my work and ideas on catatonia in autism; this has been hugely helpful in my mission to increase awareness and knowledge.

- Last but not least, the editorial team at JKP: Natalie for instigating the project, and Simeon, James and Hannah for helpful advice during different stages of book editing and production.

# Preface

I get contacted by people in the UK and from all over the world who have by chance stumbled on descriptions of autism-related catatonia and suddenly realised that there may be a name and an explanation for the deterioration in functioning, freezing episodes and other mobility, movement and speech difficulties and shutdown phenomena which has become a nightmare for their son or daughter with autism or for themselves. The stories of individuals and their families are familiar and yet different on many dimensions. The threads which run through the stories and weave the tale together include the debilitating effects, distress suffered, not being listened to or understood, misdiagnosis or no diagnosis or help from umpteen professionals seen, and a sense of isolation and hopelessness.

I was introduced to the concept of catatonia in autism by Dr Lorna Wing. As with a lot of what is widely accepted about autism today, Lorna Wing had great insight and noted the overlap between the features of autism and catatonia long before anyone else. Although initially this overlap was of academic and research interest, it was the deterioration of functioning and the exacerbation of the features of catatonia in some people with autism and the distress and stress suffered by the person concerned and their families which became our focus.

We realised quickly that even offering an explanation and an understanding of some of the perplexing symptoms and phenomena which their son or daughter showed on some days but not others, in some situations but not others, was helpful and enabled them to cope and link in to relevant services and professional help. This has recently also applied to intellectually high functioning autistic individuals, some of whom are beginning to get recognition and professional help for their long-standing catatonia-related difficulties which had been misdiagnosed, misunderstood or simply not believed.

My life-changing experiences in my clinical work in catatonia and autism happened when I met a young man whom I will refer to as Ryan. At the time, I was providing a specialist locum service to the community team for learning disabilities to advise the team on referrals of people with autism and complex challenges. Ryan was 23 years old and living with his mother who was his sole carer. At the first home visit, I was struck by Ryan's most severe presentation of chronic catatonia, the restrictive and isolated lifestyle being led by him and his mother and the sadness and hopelessness expressed by his mother who seemed resigned to the fact that there was no explanation and help for the mysterious 'illness' which had affected Ryan since he left school at 16 years of age. Ryan was painstakingly thin, sat on the sofa with his neck and head twisted, and did not speak or move. He could barely open his mouth when his mother fed him patiently and lovingly over two to three hours. There were three aspects in my work with Ryan which were very significant and relevant to writing this book.

First, Ryan had been seen by various child and adult psychiatrists, neurologists and psychologists who had all given up on him after ruling out depression (as he did not respond to antidepressant medication) and organic/neurological causes as nothing was detected on various medical tests including an EEG, MRI scan, blood tests, and so on. The fact that Ryan's diagnosis of autism-related catatonia was missed was not surprising in the mid-1990s as there was very little literature on the subject of catatonia in relation to people with autism. However, the disconcerting fact is that there is still very limited awareness and recognition of catatonia, shutdown and breakdown in autistic individuals.

The second significant aspect of working with Ryan and his mother was our realisation as to the lifeline provided to both by acknowledging, understanding and naming his 'mysterious' deterioration. This not only took away the isolation and hopelessness, but empowered them with knowledge and renewed energy and motivation to get help and services which in fact transformed Ryan's existence and life and consequently his mother's.

The third aspect about Ryan related to how he was able to respond and overcome the posture and movement difficulties of catatonia with gentle one-to-one support, verbal and physical prompts and when he worked on cognitively stimulating and challenging tasks from non-verbal psychological tests. Ryan was able to sit up, hold his head upright, and carry out smooth movements with excellent dexterity and fine motor skills. As he worked through the tasks, his whole body seemed to relax, his blank facial expression gradually transformed and his vacant eyes lit up. It was as if he gradually thawed and came alive from a semi-frozen state. He connected and engaged with the tasks with interest, motivation and concentration and smiled when I reassured him and praised his performance. I was amazed to see his response and the evidence of his 'locked' high intellectual ability. I remember calling Lorna Wing excitedly and arranged for her to see how Ryan was able to respond and how we could offer support to him and his family. This was the birth of our 'Shah and Wing' psychological approach to catatonia in autism. As we saw more individuals and their families, and also began researching catatonia in autism, it became clearer to us that the manifestation of catatonia in autism was very different from the acute and severe catatonia described in the psychiatric literature. Thus it had to be understood and managed differently, and this had to be linked in to the person's underlying autism and the reasons for their shutdown.

As I saw more and more autistic individuals with different manifestations and different levels of catatonia, I noticed their fluctuations and responses and behaviours with different external demands and situations. I became determined to use my knowledge and skills as a clinical psychologist in autism and help these individuals and their families as much as I could. I had already developed an interest in using a stress-vulnerability-breakdown model to assess autistic people with complex secondary problems and advise parents, carers, multi-disciplinary professionals, staff and service providers using a bio-psycho-ecological approach. I started applying the same approach to understanding and working with autistic individuals with catatonia and related breakdown. I was able to work with individuals, families and service providers to find pragmatic tailor-made solutions to the complex problems of managing, living with and finding help and services for a disorder which was poorly understood and accepted. I started building up a catalogue of clinical insights and strategies by working with individuals, their families and carers.

This book is not written to debate academic or theoretical aspects of catatonia in autistic people. This book is written as a practical guide for parents, carers and professionals to increase awareness, interest and recognition and to share the clinical insight and strategies using a psycho-ecological approach. I hope that the detailed descriptions of different manifestations of catatonia in autistic people and the Autism Catatonia Evaluation (ACE-S) will help with early recognition, shared conceptualisation and timely management.

To achieve my aims of writing this book, I have incorporated real-life stories of individuals with whom I have been involved professionally over the years.

I know individuals with autism and their families and friends will appreciate this book as they will be able to identify with the stories and the emotions. The book will also empower them to convince health and social care professionals and service providers and commissioners to think differently and creatively about finding and funding services and support systems. I hope that professionals and practitioners who read this book will gain new insight into the concepts of catatonia, shutdown and breakdown in autistic children and adults. This will enable them to conceptualise the presenting difficulties in a different way and incorporate the ideas and strategies in their professional practice. I am optimistic that as a result, autistic individuals and their families will experience changes in the levels of support and services, not only from a professional understanding but also from a compassionate and humanitarian perspective. I hope that researchers will be drawn to investigate this most enigmatic aspect of autism. The overlap between autism and catatonia is highly significant and too important to ignore in our quest to understand the nature of autism itself.

Finally, as the awareness and acceptance increases, I am convinced that the current prevalence estimates of catatonia in autism will continue to change and rise and many different subtypes will be identified. The story of catatonia in autism is likely to be similar to that of autism in general. I recall the meagre prevalence rates of autism estimates in the 1970s and early 1980s, and many of us experiencing the same frustration and bafflement when trying to convince health, education and social care professionals and service providers about the many manifestations and complexities of autism. My final and overarching aim of writing this book is to bring about a change in understanding, acceptance and attitude for the benefit of autistic individuals who are already suffering the devastating effects and consequences of historical misconception and to prevent this for others by raising awareness.

# Chapter 1

# Introduction

Catatonia is a complex, multifaceted disorder and there is no simple or generally accepted definition. It is easy to define and recognise when it occurs in the acute and severe form with the classic signs of immobility, absence of movement, mutism and maintenance of postures (catalepsy). However, when the catatonia is chronic, complex and associated with other conditions such as autism, it becomes much more complicated to define and recognise.

It is now well documented and established that catatonia encompasses a wide range of phenomena which can occur on its own or with a range of other conditions besides autism (Rogers 1992). Catatonia in various forms has been reported to occur in people with mood disorders (Fink and Taylor 2003), Down's syndrome (Ghaziuddin, Nassiri and Miles 2015; Worley *et al.* 2015) and various other medical and neurological disorders. Sacks (1982) has described complex catatonic phenomena in post-encephalitic patients.

There are a whole range of abnormalities of posture, movement, speech and behaviour which have been observed clinically and which are considered to be catatonic in nature by various clinicians (for example, Bush *et al.* 1996; Joseph 1992; Rogers 1992). Any of these features can occur at various levels of severity and in different combinations with varied manifestations.

Catatonia in the context of autism is complex to understand and define. It can be confusing as we are dealing with two complex spectrums in which the overt manifestations of the disorders can vary enormously both in content and severity. The additional difficulty is caused by the overlap between some of the features of catatonia and those of autism.

Catatonia has a long and complex history in the psychiatric literature. The term 'catatonia' was coined by Kahlbaum in 1874 in his book titled *Catatonia or Tension Insanity* (1973 [1874]) to refer to a distinct psychiatric syndrome. In the late 1800s and early 1900s, catatonia as a clinical condition was described and studied in children and adults by different groups of psychiatrists. There was a prolific debate with regard to classification, especially with regard to whether it was an illness in its own right or a type of schizophrenia or psychosis, or an early expression of these conditions.

During this early period, there was a growing interest in identifying and describing catatonia in children and the term 'infantile catatonia' was adopted (Kraepelin 1907 [1903]). Although comparisons are difficult, it is interesting to note that some of the cases described by Maudsley (1867) and De Sanctis (1908) may have shown a combination of autism spectrum disorder (ASD) (as we understand it now) and catatonia features.

The misconception which linked catatonia only to schizophrenia started in the early 1900s. Kraepelin (1903) described catatonia as a form of 'dementia praecox'. Bleuler (1908) coined the term 'schizophrenia' to replace Kraepelin's term 'dementia praecox' and thus catatonia became regarded as a subtype of schizophrenia. This view prevailed and became fixated in classification systems, diagnostic manuals and indeed in the minds and clinical practice of most clinicians. This was despite clinical and research evidence to the contrary (Fink and Taylor 2003).

In our clinical work, Lorna Wing and I have had difficult times trying to convince professionals who firmly believed that anyone who showed catatonia had to be schizophrenic. It was sometimes impossible to get some professionals to see that catatonia was a separate condition which could occur on its own or in other disorders. I recall Lorna Wing describing her experiences of working as a psychiatrist in long-stay mental hospitals. She was convinced that in view of what we now know about catatonia and autism many of the patients who had been given a diagnosis of catatonic schizophrenia were probably misdiagnosed. She felt that it was highly likely that some of these patients had undiagnosed autism or Asperger syndrome and had also developed catatonia rather than being schizophrenic. This has been highlighted in the research study by Nylander and Gillberg (2001) and discussed with reference to rising prevalence rates of autism by Wing and Potter (2002).

Although catatonia was increasingly being reported as occurring with other organic and medical conditions, and also as a side effect of psychiatric medications (Fink and Taylor 2003), catatonia remained linked to schizophrenia and psychoses. This was probably due to the widespread reliance on diagnostic manuals such as *Diagnostic and Statistical Manual of Mental Disorders* (DSM) and *International Classification of Diseases* (ICD) as absolute truths rather than guides for clinicians.

The first three editions of DSM (American Psychiatric Association (APA) 1952, 1968, 1980) only referred to catatonia as a form of schizophrenia. Unfortunately, even DSM-4 (APA 2000) did not reflect the wider occurrence of catatonia. In DSM-4 (APA 2000), catatonia remained linked to schizophrenia although it recognised catatonia as being associated with major mood disorders and general medical conditions.

In DSM-5 (APA 2013) catatonia is no longer considered a type of schizophrenia. The category of 'catatonic schizophrenia' subtype has been abolished together with other subtypes of schizophrenia. Catatonia in DSM-5 (APA 2013) has been simplified, made more consistent and is listed as an episode specifier in various psychotic and major mood disorders. There is an additional diagnostic category of catatonia not otherwise specified. This can be applied to catatonia in various developmental disorders including autism. However, the definition of catatonia in DSM-5 (APA 2013) is still problematic and causes practical difficulty in applying the criteria to catatonia in autism. In DSM-5 (APA 2013), catatonia is defined as the presence of at least three of the following: catalepsy, waxy flexibility, stupor, posturing, agitation, mutism, negativism, mannerisms, stereotypies, grimacing, echolalia and echopraxia. Clinicians and carers of autistic individuals will immediately realise that the latter 7 of the above list of 12 features occur frequently in autistic children and adults, and in fact are established catatonic features which overlap with autistic features (Leary and Hill 1996; Wing and Gould 1979; Wing and Shah 2006). If clinicians apply the above criteria rigidly and use only a categorical diagnostic approach and try and apply it to autistic people, there is a strong possibility that clinicians will only apply the catatonia diagnosis to the most severe cases of acute catatonia (with stupor, waxy flexibility, mutism and posturing), or wrongly apply the diagnosis of catatonia to people with autism who show the overlapping features. *Most importantly, clinicians will not recognise and diagnose the most commonly seen manifestation of catatonia in autism which is a gradual deterioration/breakdown in functioning and difficulty with voluntary movements.* Also, many high functioning individuals who show episodic catatonia-type difficulties and those showing intermittent shutdown will miss recognition and support.

The definition of catatonia and its link to schizophrenia is outdated in the ICD 10 (WHO 1992). Fortunately, in ICD 11 (WHO 2018) the definition of catatonia has been updated and allows for catatonia to be diagnosed in the context of various disorders including autism. The chapter on mental and behavioural disorders of ICD 11 (WHO 2018) is available online as a draft form for clinicians to use and comment.

In ICD 11 draft proposal (WHO 2018), catatonia is defined as the following:

> Catatonia is a marked disturbance in the voluntary control of movements characterized by several of the following: extreme slowing or absence of motor activity, mutism, purposeless motor activity unrelated to external stimuli, assumption and maintenance of rigid, unusual or bizarre postures, resistance to instructions or attempts to be moved, or automatic compliance with instructions. Catatonia may be diagnosed in the context of certain specific mental disorders, including Mood disorders, Schizophrenia, and Autism spectrum disorder.

Thus it is positive that also in ICD 11, catatonia is no longer linked only to schizophrenia and it is recognised that it can occur in the context of ASD. The defining features do not cover all the clinical manifestations of catatonia in autistic individuals. Hopefully, this will be corrected in response to comments from clinicians.

In autistic individuals, the most severe acute and classic form of catatonia as described in the psychiatric literature and the psychiatric diagnostic manuals can occur but it is rare (Billstedt, Gillberg and Gillberg 2005; Wing and Shah 2000). Manifestations of catatonia in autism are usually gradual, chronic and complex as described below. At this point in time, we do not have a complete picture of the range of manifestations of catatonia in autism as new subgroups are coming to light. Until definitions, subgroups and boundaries of overlap become clearer, it would be of heuristic value to use descriptions and methods developed in clinical practice for diagnosis and management.

# Subtypes of catatonia manifestations in autism spectrum disorder

During our extensive clinical and research studies in autism and in the overlap between the two conditions, and the development of catatonia-related deterioration and breakdown in people with ASD, we have identified the following main types of catatonia manifestations.

## 1. Chronic catatonia and catatonia-type deterioration and breakdown

This type of catatonia can be manifested in various different ways in autistic individuals. The most important defining feature is that there is a change and deterioration in the individual's ability to carry out voluntary movements and activity to the extent that it affects their daily functioning, independence, behaviour and quality of life. This type of catatonia can have a severe negative impact on the individual's life, although these individuals may not show any of the most classic signs of the acute type of catatonia such as stupor, mutism, catalepsy, waxy flexibility and posturing. Some individuals with chronic catatonia may show these aspects at a mild level and intermittently, and in some, the catatonia can progress to the most severe level with many of the classic aspects of the acute type of catatonia.

This type of chronic catatonia often occurs together with varying levels of regression of skills and independence, and with more general autistic breakdown. In fact, catatonia-related deterioration in autism can be considered one type of autistic breakdown. Autistic individuals are prone to different types of breakdown, depending on their underlying type of autism, personality and psychological profile.

## 2. Acute catatonia (general)

This type of catatonia can occur in autistic children and adults, just as it can with other mental, neurological and medical conditions. This is usually an acute condition and refers to the classic signs of catatonia. These include immobility and stupor together with mutism, catalepsy and waxy flexibility. Other classic features of catatonia such as automatic obedience, catalepsy and waxy flexibility and posturing are likely to occur as well. This type of catatonia can occur in autistic individuals and can range in the level of severity. It can progress to a most severe level requiring urgent medical services to sustain feeding, drinking and vital functions. Psychiatrists, neurologists, psychologists and other clinicians are most likely to be familiar with and recognise and diagnose this acute and general form of catatonia in autistic individuals rather than the more chronic type described above.

## 3. Catatonia as shutdown

Autistic children and adults can show a temporary shutdown of social interaction and communication at times of acute severe stress and anxiety, such as exams. In these cases, the individual gets back to normal as soon as the stressful event has passed. Many autistic individuals experience prolonged periods of shutdown, or show shutdown with other aspects of catatonia-type deterioration. Shutdown can affect the autistic individual in different ways. They may withdraw totally from the external environment, may be unable to communicate or respond, curl up in a ball, or engage only in self-initiated repetitive actions. Some individuals with the shutdown episodes may not show any movement difficulties associated with catatonia or may show these intermittently.

## 4. Episodic/lifelong catatonia-type difficulties

In many high functioning autistic individuals, catatonia may not always be a deterioration or breakdown, but can be a chronic or episodic difficulty in initiating movements and activities. This is beginning to be recognised as we get contacted by high functioning autistic individuals who are themselves linking their difficulties in initiation with catatonia. It is likely to become better recognised and as being a lot more prevalent as awareness increases and affected individuals come forward to seek confirmation of diagnosis of their difficulties and help and support which would have been denied to them previously. Autistic individuals who experience this 'episodic' catatonia are likely to be turned away by professionals and services due to disbelief. This is due to their ability to function at a high level and very well at other times in spite of problems in initiation which almost 'paralyse' them temporarily.

# 5. Catatonia features (not necessarily diagnostic of autistic catatonia)

Many of the features associated with catatonia are also characteristic of autism spectrum disorders from early childhood (Leary and Hill 1996; Wing and Attwood 1987; Wing and Shah 2006). These include features frequently occurring in autistic people such as stereotypic movements, grimacing, mild posturing, echolalia, complex repetitive movements such as spinning, and so on. *When these do not represent a deterioration or functioning or affect the person's independence or quality of life, such features can be described as part of the individual's autistic profile without additional catatonia diagnosis.*

A comprehensive range of catatonia-type features which occur frequently in autistic individuals are included in the Diagnostic Interview for Social and Communication Disorders (DISCO). This is a schedule for diagnosis of autism and related disorders and assessment of individual profile and needs (Leekam *et al.* 2002; Wing *et al.* 2002). The DISCO includes questions concerning all kinds of motor and unusual behaviours including 28 items similar to those found in lists of catatonia features. These are useful to list as many of them can occur for the first time or increase in frequency or severity during catatonic deterioration or episodes. The catatonia-type features include the following:

- movement – odd gait, poor coordination, odd hand postures, running in circles, rocking while sitting, complex body movements, walking on tiptoe, grimacing, lack of facial expression

- speech and vocalisations – immediate echolalia, delayed echolalia, odd intonation, shrieking for no reason, laughing for no reason

- eye contact – poor eye contact, sideways glances, blank look in eyes, staring

- visual fascinations – spinning objects, twisting hands near eyes, inspecting objects from different angles

- unsocial behaviour – shouting for no reason, aggressive for no reason, lack of cooperation, destructive, stripping, inappropriate personal habits (e.g. playing with saliva), hyperactivity.

We have reported the presence and frequency of these 28 catatonia-like features in autistic people, in people with learning disabilities, in people with specific language impairment, and in a group with typical development (Wing and Shah 2006). In summary, the main and interesting findings showed that there was a high frequency of catatonia-like features in people with autistic spectrum disorder. There was some tendency for improvement with age. Interestingly, many of the catatonia-like features were also found in children with learning disabilities and specific language disorders but significantly less so.

## Prelavance of catatonia in ASD

The first systemic study of prevalence of catatonia in ASD by Wing and Shah (2000) indicated that 17 per cent of autistic people aged 15 and over showed the chronic catatonia deterioration as described above. This was based on a clinic population attending a diagnostic clinic. The findings of this study are summarised in the next chapter. A similar prevalence rate was reported by the only other study (Billstedt *et al.* 2005) which used similar criteria and definition. Other studies (Breen and Hare 2017; Ghaziuddin, Dhossche and Marcotte 2012; Hutton *et al.* 2008; Ohta, Kano and Nagai 2006) have provided estimates of prevalence which range from 12 per cent to 20 per cent. The studies are not really comparable as all use different criteria, terminology and methodology. The prevalence rates reported so far for catatonia in autism provide minimal estimates and confirm that catatonia-type difficulties affect a substantial minority of autistic people. As awareness increases and different manifestations of catatonia in autistic people become identified, it is highly likely that the prevalence rates will be much higher.

The story of catatonia in autism is likely to be similar to the story of autism with prevalence rates soaring as more heterogeneous manifestations and subgroups come to light and awareness and identification increases. Even as I write this book, I am becoming more aware of extremely intelligent girls who have developed catastrophic difficulties and periods of catatonia-type shutdown at school, and in whom the diagnoses of autism and catatonia have been missed. There are likely to be significant numbers of other children and adults who are living and struggling with autism and catatonia and related breakdown without a diagnosis. Thus, the current prevalence rates are best regarded as minimum estimates for the time being.

# Chapter 2

# Manifestations of Catatonia, Shutdown and Breakdown in Autism

Lorna Wing and I first became aware of and interested in catatonia in autism during our assessments of children and adults to carry out detailed diagnostic assessments using the Diagnostic Interview for Social and Communication Disorders (DISCO) and comprehensive psychological assessment of the individual. The DISCO is based on a multi-dimensional method of diagnosis developed by Lorna Wing and Judith Gould (Wing *et al.* 2002). It is used for diagnosis and for obtaining detailed clinical profiles and additional contextual information affecting the individual with ASD. It includes several items relevant to the presence of the overlapping catatonia-type features as discussed in Chapter 1.

We realised over time that there was a clinical 'subtype' within the ASD individuals who were showing a pattern of deterioration, regression and movement difficulties associated with catatonia in the psychiatric literature. Initially, we were reluctant to refer to these difficulties under the umbrella of 'catatonia' as these individuals were not showing the classic acute and severe type of catatonia. Gradually, we became aware of individuals with similar histories and patterns of deterioration who also showed the more classic features of catatonia such as stupor, waxy flexibility and posturing. The clinical pictures and the overlaps made us realise that what we were seeing was complex catatonia phenomena manifested by individuals with ASD in various different ways with variation from day to day, and over time and different situations. We decided to refer to this group as showing 'catatonia-like deterioration', or 'catatonia-type breakdown' and later started using these terms interchangeably with 'catatonia in autism', 'autism-related catatonia' and 'autism catatonia'. At times, we have also adopted the term 'autistic catatonia' used by Hare and Malone (2004). In this book, I have used all these term interchangeably to refer to catatonia manifestations in autistic individuals.

Lorna Wing and I first drew attention to the chronic type of catatonia in people with ASD in our seminal paper titled 'Catatonia in autism spectrum disorders' (Wing and Shah 2000). This was the first systematic study of prevalence and the clinical manifestation of catatonia in ASD and its association to underlying characteristics of ASD.

Prior to that, various authors had published case reports of catatonia of the general acute type in individuals with autism (for example, Dhossche 1998; Leary and Hill 1996; Zaw et al. 1999).

Our study highlighted the gradual onset of chronic catatonia and the fact that it was a deterioration of functioning and behaviour and the different ways in which the underlying key features of catatonia could affect individuals with ASD. The details of the study and the results are given in the paper (Wing and Shah 2000) published in *The British Journal of Psychiatry*. The main findings were as follows:

- Catatonia-like deterioration was shown in 17 per cent of those aged 15 and over in the clinic population studied. These individuals showed an obvious and a marked deterioration in movements, pattern of activities and in self-care and practical skills compared to previous levels.

- The level of severity and the actual manifestation of the catatonia features and difficulties varied in different individuals. Some needed prompts on some days and in some situations to carry out movements and activities. Others had become very prompt dependent and needed prompts on a daily basis for nearly all activities. A few individuals had to be physically supported and showed severe regression in physical and motor independence.

- Individuals who showed the catatonia-like deterioration were statistically more likely to have an underlying 'passive' type of social impairment on the scale of social impairment defined by Wing and Gould (1979). Those with catatonia-like deterioration were also statistically more likely to be impaired in expressive language before the onset of the deterioration.

- Interestingly, the following factors were not significantly associated with catatonia-like deterioration: age, gender, IQ, diagnostic subgroup (autism or Asperger syndrome) and history of epilepsy.

- Although the individuals concerned could not describe their difficulties or possible causes, many parents suggested a variety of precipitating causes such as stress of school exams, bereavement, loss of routine, structure and occupation after leaving school, difficulties of puberty and adolescence.

## Catatonia, shutdown and breakdown: Detailed description of manifestations

Since this original study, we have continued to see a vast number of autistic individuals with chronic catatonia both in our clinical practice and as part of our research studies. We have been able to define the underlying features and the manifestations seen in more detail. This section is divided into three parts:

- primary difficulties and manifestations

- secondary difficulties and autism breakdown

- consequences for the individuals and their families.

### Primary difficulties and manifestations

1. Increased slowness

2. Movement difficulties (freezing and getting stuck)

3. Movement abnormalities

4. Prompt dependence

5. Passivity and apparent lack of motivation

6. Posturing

7. Periods of shutdown

8. Catatonic excitement

9. Fluctuations of difficulty

# 1. Increased slowness

This is often (though not always) the first indication of the onset of catatonia-type breakdown. The slowness compared to the individual's normal pace is noticeable particularly during:

- walking
- verbal responses to any questions
- response to an instruction
- self-care activities such as dressing, eating, toilet use
- mealtimes.

The individual may find it difficult to keep up with the pace of a group. There are often periods of inactivity or immobility between actions which appears as slowness; for example, they may stand still for a time before beginning to walk, or stop and stand motionless during the course of walking before restarting again. During mealtimes the individual may appear to stare into space and take long breaks between each mouthful.

# 2. Movement difficulties

These can affect any voluntary movement and show as difficulty in initiating or stopping movement, and 'freezing' during movements or mid-action. The most commonly seen manifestations include the following:

- **Difficulty in initiating movement** – this can be very obvious or subtle. The person may have difficulty lifting their foot to start walking, or at particular transitions such as steps or getting off or on pavements. The person may remain standing or sitting and not be able to get up from the chair or the car seat, for instance. During mealtimes, the person may stare at the food but be unable to get started on eating. In some people the difficulty affects their ability to get out of bed and to get started on morning routines. The difficulty in initiating movement can affect any voluntary movement. Some individuals are unable to open their eyes voluntarily and their eyelids remain shut intermittently.

- **Freezing or becoming 'stuck'** – the individual may stop in the middle of carrying out an action/movement or activity. The length of 'freezing' may vary from a few seconds to several minutes before the movement is resumed. The person may 'freeze' mid-action, for example holding a toothbrush or hairbrush and starting the action, but suddenly stop mid-air as if 'frozen'. Sometimes, the freezing prevents the person from carrying out an activity, for example getting up in time to go to the toilet. The freezing can happen at any time, and people have got stuck on the toilet for hours, or been unable to get out of bed, which is often interpreted as 'laziness' or 'lack of cooperation' or a 'challenging behaviour difficulty'.

  Some individuals, especially those who are high functioning, seem to get stuck 'mentally' and develop repetitive thought patterns and mental rituals and become locked in these. In some individuals, the 'mental freezing' can occur together with 'physical freezing' or separately on its own. There may be an increase in severity of repetitive movements, repetitive and ritualistic behaviours and thoughts, and/or an onset or increase in irrational fears.

- **Hesitations and to and fro movements** – the person concerned may show hesitation in movements and actions, or make several to and fro movements before completing an action. For example, they may move their hand forwards and backwards in their attempts to pick up an object/cup of tea, and so on. The individual may walk to and fro several times before finally walking forwards.

- **Difficulty crossing thresholds/transitions** – the person concerned may stop, hesitate or walk to and fro before going through doorways, or when transitioning between different walking surfaces, for example, when walking from a paved road onto a rough road, from a carpeted floor onto a non-carpeted surface, when coming across stairs, or at the kerb while crossing the road and being unable to step off the kerb onto the road.

- **Difficulty stopping a movement or action once started** – this may appear like a ritual or prolonged routine, or sudden perseverance at any task to a point of exhaustion.

- **Effects on speech** – the movement difficulties can affect speech content, fluency and volume. Often, someone who has been able to speak fluently and communicate well starts talking in a whisper or hesitates a lot (which appears like a stutter), or generally talks and communicates a lot less than previously. Speech difficulties can progress to severe levels until the person becomes mute either all the time or in certain situations.

- **Eating and drinking difficulties** – these may include general slowness, difficulty in the movements required to eat with a fork and a knife, or inability to complete the movement smoothly. The movements required for chewing and swallowing often get affected. The individual may hold the food in their mouth for a long time, or eat very small amounts, or in some cases become unable to chew or swallow. The consequences of these can be very severe and worrying, for example, unexplainable weight loss, lack of nutrition and obvious threats to health and wellbeing. Eating and drinking difficulties and weight loss can be serious complications of catatonia and need to be monitored.

- Spending a long time in one place – this could be in the toilet, bathroom or bedroom compared to previously, for example. This may be related to actual difficulty in getting up from the toilet seat, getting out of the bath or leaving the bedroom. In some cases, this may be linked to an onset of new or increased ritualistic behaviours which interfere with carrying out smooth and normal movements and activities.

## 3. Movement abnormalities

These include various repetitive movements as seen in Tourette's syndrome, parkinsonian-type motor problems, dystonic movements, and repetitive movements affecting the extra-pyramidal system. Some occur as side effects of psychiatric medications. Autistic people who have never been on psychiatric medication can also show any of the following during a breakdown associated with catatonia. This is not surprising as various authors (e.g. Rogers 1992 and Lishman 1998) have emphasised the overlap of the features of Parkinsonism and dyskinesia with those of catatonia.

The most common movement abnormalities seen include the following:

- sudden jerky movements, tremors, involuntary movements, jumping, unusual arm movements
- blinking and/or grimacing and repetitive jaw movements
- sudden flexion of arm or leg
- posture abnormalities such as twisting head and neck and/or upper torso in seemingly awkward and uncomfortable ways
- adopting unusual postures such as crouching
- adopting and getting locked in postures, for example standing on one leg, holding the arm up for long periods
- not using both arms as previously
- increase in repetitive movements
- onset of new/bizarre movement sequences.

## 4. Prompt dependence

The person concerned may be unable to perform some or any type of movement or activity or be unable to move from one activity to another, or be unable to change posture without an external prompt. For example, while eating, the person may stop between mouthfuls until a verbal or physical prompt is given. A person who previously travelled independently may sit on a chair and be unable to get up in time to catch the bus or train, and thus be late or miss events altogether.

## 5. Passivity and apparent lack of motivation

The individual concerned appears unmotivated and unwilling to participate in activities, including those previously enjoyed. This may be due to the difficulties in carrying out voluntary activities and movements, increased passivity, and sometimes difficulty in responding to requests and in making choices and decisions. The overt manifestations may include the following:

- unwillingness to get out of bed in the morning

- reluctance to participate in daily activities

- refusal to go out (especially if asked rather than directed)

- increased periods of doing nothing

- reluctance to carry out daily routines such as bathing, shaving, dressing.

## 6. Posturing

Some individuals show the classic catatonia feature of becoming stuck or locked into postures, sometimes for hours. For example, the person concerned may stand still in one position staring into space, or with an arm or leg in an awkward position, or they may squat or crouch on the floor and be unable to come out of the posture for a long time. Some individuals show odd posture phenomena such as 'catatonic pillow'. When this occurs the person seems unable to put their head down on the pillow and can remain stuck for hours in a most uncomfortable lying position with their head raised a few inches from the pillow.

## 7. Periods of shutdown

Some individuals may show short or prolonged periods of shutdown, sometimes intermittently with any of the other difficulties listed above. Shutdown refers to the individual withdrawing and being unresponsive and uncommunicative. Some individuals curl up or stay in bed and appear cut off from everything around them.

## 8. Catatonic excitement

This can be manifested in a number of ways, but is always episodic and short lasting. During an episode, various behaviours may be shown. These include:

- uncontrollable and frenzied movements, for example hitting out at people or objects, or themselves (e.g. chin slapping), running aimlessly (some self-injurious behaviours may fall into this category)

- uncontrollable and often bizarre vocalisations

- experiences of sensory or perceptual distortions

- uncharacteristic outburst of aggression or destruction, for example, an individual who has become totally inactive and passive may get up suddenly and throw or smash something and then sit down passively again.

## 9. Fluctuations of difficulty

One of the most intriguing, puzzling and unexplainable aspects of autism-related catatonia is the fluctuations in severity and pattern of difficulties on different days and situations. On good days, an individual may experience fewer difficulties with movements and may be able to perform more fluid, smooth movements without freezing. On a bad day, the same individual may have severe difficulties getting out of bed in the morning, and continue to have difficulties with initiating and completing movements.

Sometimes, some external situation seems to provide a temporary ability to overcome the 'block', and the individual is able to perform an activity or interact and communicate smoothly without becoming stuck. For example, one young autistic man with catatonia who used to take three to four hours to complete his morning routines and get dressed was able to overcome this and was the first person to be ready on the day his brother was getting married!

In some individuals, a sudden 'emergency' can act as a stimulus which enables them to overcome the catatonia temporarily. Lorna Wing and I came across one young man who had become wheelchair bound. One day, when this young man's father was about to fall, the young man was able to get up from his wheelchair at lightning speed and save his father from falling.

I sometimes find that on the day of my assessment, some individuals function better and are able to complete non-verbal psychometric tests without showing the catatonia-related difficulties. Their parents and carers report how much more 'catatonic' the individual had been before and after my visit. Although it is tempting to take the credit, I do not think that it is my personal presence or some special psychological power in myself or my tools which has this positive temporary effect. It seems more to do with new stimulation, structured external demands and gentle one-to-one prompting, which enables them to function without freezing.

Such day-to-day and situational fluctuations make it difficult for others to understand this perplexing disorder. Sometimes, professionals and carers feel that the individual is in control of the catatonia, or that they are being stubborn, wilful or lazy rather than having genuine difficulties and inability to initiate movements and carry out voluntary activities. Some professionals do not believe parental reports about the difficulties which the individual has been showing. It is important that professionals listen carefully to the whole story and not jump to conclusions on the basis of how the individual presents during an assessment.

---

## Secondary difficulties and autism breakdown

1. Social withdrawal and communication problems

2. Decline in self-help skills

3. Incontinence

4. 'Challenging' behaviour

5. Mobility and muscle wastage

6. Physical problems

7. Breakdown

---

The effects of the catatonia-related breakdown and all the possible primary difficulties described above can be devastating for the person concerned due to the secondary effects and challenges. These occur frequently as the catatonia-related breakdown is not picked up in early stages, but only when the secondary effects and a more general breakdown set in, and there are obvious changes to the person's functioning, skills, independence, participation and quality of life. The most common secondary effects include the following.

## 1. Social withdrawal and communication problems

Some individuals who had previously enjoyed family get-togethers and social occasions are no longer able to do so. Family, friends and carers find it more difficult to get through to them and engage them in conversation.

## 2. Decline in self-help skills

Individuals who have been totally independent in self-help skills can become semi-dependent or fully dependent on carers for basic self-care needs due to the effects of movement difficulties, in particular lack of initiation, passivity, regression of skills, and lack of focus and interest in normal activities.

## 3. Incontinence

This is often due to the person being unable to get up from the chair or from the bed to get to the toilet, and being unable to ask for help due to the catatonia. This can progress to a more general incontinence.

## 4. 'Challenging' behaviour

This can occur due to the frustration about the catatonic difficulties and the changes which this entails.

## 5. Mobility and muscle wastage

Many autistic individuals who develop catatonia-related breakdown become immobile and inactive for long periods. This can cause muscle wasting and various secondary mobility and physical problems. We know of individuals who are now permanently in a wheelchair due to the secondary muscle wasting.

## 6. Physical problems

This can include difficulty in passing urine, severe weight loss and amenorrhoea. Although rare, severe catatonia can sometimes affect breathing, and the person may hold their breath for long periods, and have a distorted pattern of breathing.

## 7. Breakdown

Some individuals show additional difficulties characteristic of autism breakdown. This may include an overall exacerbation of their autism, for example, increased social and communication difficulties and increased repetitive activities and rituals. Their tolerance and resilience may be decreased so they get more easily distressed, irritated, angry, frustrated and anxious which may result in inappropriate or 'challenging behaviour' and/or self-injurious behaviour. In some individuals, the breakdown decreases their level of concentration, focus, engagement and enjoyment. In some individuals, their tolerance for others' demands decreases and they start showing a pattern of 'demand resistance' characteristics.

---

### Consequences for the individuals and their families

1. Inability to attend school, college or work, or cope with everyday life
2. Stress for families and carers

---

## 1. Inability to attend school, college or work, or cope with everyday life

This can be a common secondary consequence of autism-related catatonia and many high functioning people have given up and been unable to achieve their potential or lead meaningful lives due to the difficulties of autism-related catatonia. There is invariably a decline in the quality of life, both for the individual and family members.

## 2. Stress for families and carers

The additional stress and worry experienced by carers and families of autistic individuals who develop catatonia cannot be underestimated. On top of everything else, individuals and their families have to constantly confront disbelieving professionals and be labelled as 'demanding', 'uncooperative' and so on.

## Assessment of autism catatonia

There are various published rating scales for the assessment of catatonic symptoms in psychiatric patients. These include the Rogers Scale (Rogers 1992), the modified Rogers Scale (Starkstein *et al.* 1996), the Bush-Francis Catatonia Rating Scale (Bush *et al.* 1996) and the Catatonia Rating Scale (Braunig *et al.* 2000). These scales have been developed for general catatonia and are not appropriate for screening for or assessing the type of catatonia manifestations which are clinically seen in autistic individuals. The main difficulty with using such catatonia scales for autistic individuals is that many of the features listed in these scales are also characteristic of autistic spectrum disorders from very early childhood.

There are no specific rating scales available for the assessment of autism-related catatonia. Breen and Hare have developed a questionnaire called the 'attenuated behaviour questionnaire' based on Wing and Shah's (2000) clinical descriptions of catatonia features and catatonia-like deterioration (Breen and Hare 2017). This has been used as a research tool to identify the presence of catatonic features and autism catatonia but would have limited use as a clinical questionnaire for the assessment of autism-related catatonia. The complex manifestations of catatonia, shutdown and breakdown described above cannot be assessed by a categorical approach using checklists and general rating scales. The author of this book has developed an assessment schedule for this purpose specifically. This is described in the next section.

## Autism Catatonia Evaluation (ACE-S)
### Description
The ACE-S has been designed and developed in clinical practice by the present author. It is published in Appendix 1 in this book for ease of reference and use. It is a framework for collecting relevant information for autistic children and adults in whom catatonia, shutdown and/or related breakdown are suspected. It can be used by anyone (carers, parents, autistic individuals, practitioners and professionals) as a tool to collect relevant information to build an individual profile. The ACE-S is based on the concepts of catatonia, shutdown and breakdown described in this book. It can be used by anyone involved with an autistic individual in whom catatonia, shutdown and/or autism breakdown is suspected or as a screening tool for these aspects during other mental and physical health assessments.

## Uses

The ACE-S can be used for the following purposes:

- to guide assessment, recognition and diagnosis of catatonia, shutdown and breakdown in autistic individuals

- to describe and evaluate catatonia manifestations in autistic individuals

- to establish baselines and monitor progress

- to plan strategies, support and services and inform care plans

- for research purposes.

## Instructions for use and caution

The ACE-S is not a quick diagnostic checklist for categorical assessments, and it is not suitable for quantitative evaluation. It is a dimensional framework for collecting information in a systematic way to build up an overall picture of the manifestations of catatonia, shutdown and breakdown in autistic individuals.

The ACE-S is not suitable for a direct assessment of the individual at a given point in time. It cannot be used to elicit the information by interviewing the person concerned or getting them to demonstrate the catatonia manifestations. Users need to be aware that there can be a lot of variation in the amount of difficulty shown by the individual on different days and in different situations. Thus, it is essential for users to get information about the individual from a variety of sources to get a full picture.

The ACE-S should be completed by using information from individuals, parents, carers, teachers and others who have known the person and are able to give an overview of their functioning, deterioration and difficulties in different situations. This can be supplemented by information from direct observation of the individual in different settings, video footage and psychological assessment to build up the whole picture. Information from multi-disciplinary assessments such as speech and language therapy assessment and occupational therapy assessment can also be useful to supplement the information for particular sections.

## The Autism Catatonia Evaluation (ACE-S)

The ACE-S consists of the following sections. (The full version is given in Appendix 1.)

Section A – Deterioration (Independence, Speech, Activity)

Section B – Movement Difficulty and Shutdown

Section C – Movement and Behaviour Abnormalities

Section D – Overlapping Catatonia/Autism Features

Section E – Autism Breakdown

Section F – Secondary Difficulties

# Chapter 3

# Different Lives – Similar Stories

The real-life descriptions below of the manifestations of catatonia and related difficulties/breakdown are all based on individuals known to and assessed by the author. The names and some details have been changed to preserve anonymity and confidentiality. The ages in brackets next to each name refer to their age at the time of referral to the author.

## Barry (23-year-old male)

Barry had a diagnosis of high functioning autism from childhood. He had attended a mainstream school, was able to travel on public transport independently, enjoyed reading and communicated fluently. He enjoyed family events and impressed people with his factual knowledge on various topics of interest. He started showing a pattern of regression, deterioration and freezing episodes after leaving school and attending a mainstream college. Barry's parents felt totally devastated by his deterioration as they had come to terms with his autism, but this was totally unexpected and difficult to make sense of. Barry was seen by various professionals including a psychiatrist (for two years), neurologists, psychologists and an occupational therapist. He had all possible medical investigations including blood tests, an EEG and an MRI scan. These did not show any physical abnormalities. He had been discharged without any diagnosis or help provided to him or the family. By chance, Barry's parents read an article on catatonia in autism and got the GP to refer Barry to a renowned specialist tertiary autism service. Barry's catatonia was not diagnosed and he was discharged with the conclusion that he had adult autism, and his parents were left to cope with his increasing deterioration and dependency. None of the professionals concerned had linked his pattern of deterioration to autism-related catatonia, and moreover had blatantly dismissed his mother's enquiry whether the likelihood of catatonia affecting Barry should be considered. Had the catatonia been recognised at an early stage or if his mother had been listened to, Barry's life story and quality of life and that of his family would have been different to what it is likely to be now.

On the basis of a detailed assessment and observations, I was able to conceptualise his difficulties and 'odd', 'bizarre' behaviours as the following manifestations of catatonia and related breakdown:

1. Movement difficulties – Barry tended to hesitate and show repetitive to and fro movements before completing an action such as picking up an object. He tended to stop and walked forwards and backwards several times before crossing door thresholds and transitions such as stepping off the kerb.

2. Movement abnormalities – Barry showed a whole range of 'odd' movements and postures such as holding his arms in a particular odd posture, spinning around and crouching. He also showed sudden jerky and involuntary movements including random frowning and grimacing and odd repetitive vocalisations. Barry also showed difficulties in stopping an action and had a tendency to persevere with an activity until asked to stop.

3. Prompt dependency – Barry needed one-to-one support and prompting to finish an activity, or to carry on with walking or an action when he stopped midway. He also started requiring prompting for getting out of bed and all self-care activities.

4. Getting stuck and/or freezing episodes – Barry became stuck and 'frozen' in physical ways and also in his thinking and communication. This could be momentary or longer, and could happen quite suddenly in the middle of a sentence or while doing a task. When his thought processes got 'stuck', he appeared to be 'switched off' and seemed to be staring blankly. He appeared disconnected from his environment. If this happened during communication, he stopped and then struggled to speak and repeated the same words over and over again. Yet, when he was not having a 'freezing' episode, he could talk very fluently with good articulation and meaning.

## Secondary effects

The secondary difficulties affected Barry's quality of life, and also put huge strain and stress on his parents trying to care for him and support him at home without appropriate professional help, guidance or support.

Barry had become more withdrawn and family and friends found it more difficult to get through to him, and to engage him in communication. These difficulties fluctuated depending on the situation and the demands being made on him. He functioned best in a one-to-one structured situation.

Barry's independence at home and outside in the community and enjoyment with family were compromised and this had a restrictive and negative impact on his quality of life. He could not be left unsupervised to carry out tasks in the kitchen, or go out by himself.

Barry was showing difficulties with chewing and swallowing due to movement difficulties associated with catatonia. Barry went through periods of not eating enough and had lost a significant amount of weight.

## Ketan (24-year-old male)

Ketan was referred to us after an autism practitioner providing one-to-one support had the insight to suspect that Ketan was showing symptoms of catatonia which could explain the severe deterioration in his functioning with loss of skills and regression.

Ketan too had had many medical investigations and interventions including MRI scans, CT scans, changes to epilepsy medication, blood tests and EEG. These had been performed at the local hospital and also the National Hospital for Neurology and Neurosurgery. Ketan had also had a three-day assessment at a specialist assessment centre. All of the results had come back as normal, and none of the umpteen professionals and experts had spotted or mentioned the possibility of catatonia.

When I assessed Ketan, he was showing the full picture of autism catatonia and related breakdown with all the characteristic manifestations including the following:

1. Movement difficulties and prompt dependency – These included hesitations and difficulties in completing actions,

stopping while walking, and hands locked in a position. At times, Ketan needed a prompt even to lift his foot to start walking.

2. Movement abnormalities – Ketan showed sudden jerky movements, tremors, involuntary movements, jumping, unusual arm movements, grimacing, and repetitive jaw movements.

3. Slow and robotic – Ketan had become slow in all movements and seemed robotic in his actions without smooth fluidity of movement.

4. Getting stuck and/or freezing episodes – Ketan had episodes of freezing, for example, being unable to get out of bed, freezing at the top of stairs and needing two people to support him to come down stairs.

5. Regression in skills and speech – Ketan was showing a regression in various skills. His language, which had been fluent previously, had deteriorated to a level of just odd vocalisations and being mostly mute. On a couple of occasions, Ketan had come out with a whole sentence, especially during severe frustration. My assessment indicated that his receptive vocabulary was still intact, but it was the expressive communication which had been affected by the catatonia.

6. Catatonic excitement – Ketan had episodes of catatonic excitement, which led to bizarre uncharacteristic behaviours, for example, leaving the house unexpectedly, leaving the front door open and going missing for hours. He was also found stuck at the top of the road near home and was unable to move until assisted.

## Secondary effects

There were secondary effects which were impacting on Ketan's functioning and behaviour. The family was at breaking point with the stress and distress of not knowing what was happening to Ketan, and why none of the professionals could throw any light on his continuing deterioration and difficulties.

Ketan had become increasingly withdrawn and non-communicative. He had also developed chewing and swallowing difficulties and as a result had lost over three stones in weight. He had difficulty passing urine at times which seemed related to the catatonia as all physical causes had been eliminated. (I have come across other people with catatonia who have difficulty passing urine and are helped by being given a verbal prompt.)

## Nina (13-year-old female)

Nina was a young girl with a diagnosis of autism and severe learning difficulty. She was described as a girl with a sparkle and a smile and bringing joy to all who knew her. She loved singing and had perfect pitch. She loved school, home, routine and being around people, and had a great capacity to live for the moment and enjoy everything that life offered her. She was in the 'passive' group and happily engaged with life and activities organised by others. Nina had a fascination with Lourdes in France, which she had enjoyed visiting regularly with her parents.

Nina's life started changing with the onset of puberty and change to senior school. She became less tolerant to stress and changes and started becoming withdrawn and uncommunicative. Her smile disappeared and she gradually began to need prompting. There were also increased demands at school due to a change-over to senior class with changes of teachers and routines. Unfortunately, the early signs of Nina's onset of catatonia and related breakdown were not recognised. Nina continued to deteriorate, and started having increased periods of time out of school resulting in further loss of routine, structure and stimulation. Various psychiatric medications were tried, but these only increased the severity of her catatonia.

It seemed a most cruel stroke of fate and combination of factors which took away Nina's smile, her singing, sparkle and joy of living. For me, the saddest aspect was the lack of early recognition of her difficulties and the negative effects of the trial and error experimentation with powerful psychiatric drugs which was unwarranted.

Gradually, Nina deteriorated and showed a cyclical pattern of catatonia which oscillated between severe and moderate. At the time of being referred to me at the age of 13 years, Nina was no longer at school due to her immobility and inability to initiate movement and carry out any activity. On reviewing the documented information about the onset and pattern and manifestation of the catatonia, it was clear that over a period of two years, Nina had shown nearly every feature associated with autism-related catatonia and also shown the most severe catatonia episodes of going into catatonic stupor and then gradually coming out of it. The main phenomena relating to catatonia and the related breakdown shown by Nina over the two-year period had included the following:

1. Social and communication aspects – Nina showed increased passivity, increased social withdrawal, and partial and total mutism. Given Nina's personality and interest in positive engagement with others, it was highly likely that the catatonia made it impossible for her to engage with others and express herself.

2. Movement difficulties – Nina showed the whole range including:

   i. hesitations and sudden jerky movements

   ii. freezing during actions and in postures

   iii. chewing and swallowing difficulties

   iv. locked jaw and mouth

   v. twisting neck and head and remaining stuck in an awkward position

   vi. eyes remaining shut for periods of time (I have come across this distressing aspect of catatonia in other people too)

   vii. periods of catatonic stupor which had required hospitalisation.

3. Prompt dependence – This increased to a severe level whereby Nina was unable to carry out any action or movement without physical and/or verbal prompts.

4. Catatonic excitement/impulsive behaviour – Nina showed episodes of totally uncharacteristic behaviour including hitting out, screaming, uncontrollable laughter and taking off her clothes.

## Secondary effects

These included:

- regression of skills, lack of focus and interest in normal activities

- onset of and increase in obsessional behaviours and increased sensitivity and intolerance of particular aspects of the environment

- secondary medical difficulties including severe weight loss, severe constipation and amenorrhoea.

The possible cumulative 'causes' for Nina's catatonia, shutdown and breakdown are described in Chapter 5.

## Chloe (19-year-old female)

Chloe is an amazing girl who has bravely faced and fought the torment and suffering due to developing catatonia and related breakdown. She has been misunderstood, misdiagnosed and treated with medication which has put her in total catatonic stupor (luckily reversed after timely withdrawal of the medication). Chloe has been able to write and talk about her subjective experiences during episodes of catatonia. This has given me tremendous insight and helped my understanding of catatonia in more able people like Chloe, and also in autistic people who do not have or have lost the capacity to use speech to describe their experiences and feelings. I was most struck by Chloe's descriptions of the intense emotions she experienced internally but being unable to show or express these outwardly during her catatonia episodes. I had often wondered about this during my encounters with autistic people with or without catatonia who were unable to express any emotion or feelings. Chloe confirmed my clinical intuition that most of them probably experience strong internal emotions and feelings, but have difficulty understanding and expressing them. Through her determination and courage and her family's help, Chloe has overcome and learnt coping strategies for her difficulties and is pursuing her life goals.

Chloe had been diagnosed with Asperger syndrome since the age of four. She first showed symptoms of catatonia together with a complex mental health breakdown from the age of eight years, and had since suffered from many different and varying levels of catatonia intermittently at different times.

Her manifestation of catatonia was of the type often seen in high functioning autistic people who are able to talk about their experiences:

1.  Being stuck in repetitive routines, rituals or thoughts – These could occur any time and could last for hours. Chloe had experienced these debilitating and severe phenomena in various ways over the years. Some recent rituals had included getting in and out of bed repeatedly to fix her hair, cleaning rituals, repeatedly going in and out of the bathroom, and so on. During some of these episodes, Chloe also experienced thought repetition and becoming preoccupied by a loop of repetitive thoughts which she could not get out of.

    Chloe had written quite vivid descriptions of times when she had become stuck. She often described overwhelming internal emotion and anxiety at these times, but outwardly did not show emotion but became stuck in thoughts, actions or repetitive routines. The following is an example of Chloe's descriptions:

    > When frozen, my mind is most likely to be fuzzy with being stuck in the midst of whatever is causing it or at worst, in a state of intense anxiety. This of course is very stressful for me, especially when I have got drawn into something that I may have been fearful of happening beforehand. There is simply nothing else occupying my head apart from these thoughts and whatever I am stuck trying to do. As for my body, most of it will be at a standstill, other than the parts that I am compelled to move. If I have been frozen for ages, I will become either numb or aching, if any parts of my body are out of their default position.

2.  Posturing – Chloe could become stuck in one posture or in one position for days! At these times, she was fully conscious but was unable to move and got frozen in one position and posture.

3.  Full blown catatonia – Chloe had an episode of full blown catatonia which started off mildly. This was treated with an increase in her risperidone medication, which seemed to trigger the full blown catatonia causing stupor, muteness

and total inability to move. Fortunately, the link between the increase in the medication and the catatonia was realised and the risperidone was withdrawn. Chloe was then gradually able to come out of the catatonic state, and recover.

4. Fluctuation between over-arousal and excitability and catatonic states – From childhood, Chloe had shown a marked tendency to react disproportionately to sensory stimuli, emotional arousal and anything she perceived as negative. She could become overwhelmed by sensory or emotional overload. She tended to react in two extreme ways. She could become hyper-aroused, excitable and impulsive. At the other extreme, she could become stuck in rituals or go into catatonic states.

5. Situational fluctuations – Chloe could be stuck in a totally repetitive activity such as picking up fluff from the carpet and would be unresponsive. However, when external professionals visited her to assess her, she would respond to their requests (on one occasion also going out shopping with a professional), but resuming the same position and repetitive activity for hours afterwards. Many of the professionals questioned the authenticity of her difficulties of catatonia due to such observations, and misjudged and misdiagnosed her as a result.

Chloe is passionate and determined about wanting to help others understand autism catatonia. The following extract from statements recorded by her explains what she has been through in her words:

The actual experience of catatonia is just too frightening to be able to describe and to put into words properly. It's just an intensely debilitating condition that cannot be underestimated in any way at all.

I was unable to eat or talk during the crisis and I could only drink whilst being aided by my mum and could go to the toilet but I had to be guided to the bathroom and back.

The consequences and the aftermath of catatonia are very severe and unfortunately it took me a long time to recover from the emotional and psychological aftermath of the last catatonic episode I suffered from.

As a child I missed out on a lot of school and swimming from when I had the catatonia, both of which I fell behind in.

Then in the more recent years when I was 18 I missed out on two exams and a school trip to Italy and my Leavers Ball, all of which upset me a lot because these are opportunities I am unlikely to be able to experience again.

I hope this has helped you understand more about this serious and complex condition. It's not something that we can control whatsoever.

## Akash (33-year-old male)

Akash was a young man who was highly intelligent and had a late diagnosis of Asperger syndrome. Akash had attended mainstream school where he had suffered severe stress and anxiety and had been a victim of severe bullying. At the age of 19 after leaving school, Akash had a severe breakdown of behaviour and was admitted to a psychiatric hospital.

A diagnosis of Asperger syndrome was finally made and a range of behavioural and psychiatric drug treatments were tried. None of these had any positive effects on Akash. Akash expressed himself with alacrity and deep feelings in letters to his parents. He resented the controlling regime and felt threatened, abused and distressed by the behavioural treatments which included seclusion and time-out. Akash's onset of catatonia seemed linked to these stresses and the side effects of the neuroleptic medication. There were descriptions of Akash showing movement difficulties, freezing episodes and catatonic excitement characterised by marked agitation, anxiety and frenzied repetitive movements.

After this time at the psychiatric hospital, Akash seemed to lose his spirit and fight and it was as if he gave in and shut down. He deteriorated gradually and was showing severe catatonia by the time I assessed him a few years later. It was sad and distressing to see what had become of a young man who had taken pride in his appearance, had high intelligence, eloquent language and expression and a strong spirit. He was locked inside himself and seemed resigned to his fate. The look of despair and sadness in his eyes spoke volumes, but alas no one understood him! His day-to-day difficulties due to catatonia are described below in the hope that others like him are saved from such a terrible fate.

# 1. Mobility and movement

Akash was a lot stiffer in his movement and mobility on some days than others. On some days, he was slower and stiffer from the moment he woke up, and everything was laborious and required a lot of effort. On other days he required less prompting and was more fluid in his movements.

Akash walked slowly with his head bowed down and his arms held stiffly by his side. He showed various uncontrolled repetitive movements and posture and gait abnormalities. He needed prompting to go anywhere. Once he started walking, he was able to follow and carried on until his escort stopped. He then stopped as well and needed further verbal prompting to walk again.

Akash needed physical help to get out of bed due to difficulties in initiating the movement required to move his legs to the edge of the bed. If he was not woken up or helped out of bed, he would just lie there. He was not able to call staff to come to him. This was true of various people I assessed, and I wondered whether Akash too had been regarded as 'lazy', 'manipulative' and wilful – descriptions I had heard too often from well-meaning care staff and other professionals who could not understand the fluctuating nature of the catatonia. I wondered and often tried to imagine how people like Akash would have felt: trapped and imprisoned and unable to communicate their distress, ask for help or explain their terrible predicament. I could empathise and sympathise but I doubt that I would ever be able to fully understand their anguish or imagine how life would actually feel for them.

# 2. Regression in self-care skills

Akash's difficulties in movement affected all his self-care skills. For someone who had been fully independent and liked his privacy and personal space, it must have been humiliating to have to forgo all personal pride and dignity and be totally dependent on others, even for the most intimate personal hygiene aspects. I wondered whether this was more difficult for Akash to bear or for his parents to witness.

# 3. Eating and drinking

The movement difficulties being experienced by Akash were affecting his eating, and could only be ascertained by careful observation.

He took a very long time to eat because of the difficulty in initiating and completing movements required for feeding himself with a fork and knife. I observed him eating a meal on two different occasions, and the variability of the control of his movements was apparent. On the first day when I observed him, Akash spent over half an hour before he got his first spoonful of dessert on the spoon. He was trying, but was having difficulty completing the action. Thus, to the observer, it looked as if he was playing around or hesitating or not wanting his food. On the second occasion I observed him, he showed some hesitation of movement, but was able to get a mouthful after about the third attempt. When Akash got stuck on his movement during eating, he also got triggered into a lot of ritualistic repetitive behaviours such as touching the food lightly with his finger and pushing it. Akash appeared to have a lot of difficulty at times with the movements required to take food off the fork or spoon and to chew and swallow food. It was not surprising that Akash had lost interest in food and hardly ever finished the meals. If only staff and carers could have understood his difficulties and the frustration and made eating easier for him. It seemed strange to me that the staff who were so concerned about Akash's independence (and hence reluctant to help him) could not understand why he needed help now so desperately to regain his independence and quality of life.

## 4. Communication and social interaction

At the time of my assessment, Akash did not communicate meaningfully. All his speech consisted of repetitive phrases. He was not able to communicate even basic needs verbally. For someone who had been able to communicate with alacrity, insight and emotion, it was extremely sad to witness his inability to express any needs, thoughts, feelings and wishes. Akash's eyes, alive with a soulful sadness, seemed to suggest that he was listening and watching intently as if trying to understand.

It was difficult to estimate how much Akash was able to understand, and his carers assumed that he understood very little as he was so uncommunicative. However, in view of his past capacity for understanding language, I estimated that he probably understood a lot more than he was able to communicate himself. This was borne out by a non-verbal test of comprehension of words and concepts. Akash's comprehension of language and intelligence was intact so he could understand what was happening, but was locked inside himself, unable to express his thoughts, wishes and feelings.

Akash used to be confident and enjoyed social interaction with familiar people. Sadly, since the onset of the catatonia, Akash had stopped interacting at all with other people. He stood or sat around quietly observing but not interacting.

Akash's pattern of activity and difficulties fluctuated a lot on different days. On some days, he was a lot more at ease, and required fewer prompts to do things. On other days, he needed to be prompted into action by verbal instruction, verbal prompts, physical prompts and physical assistance. These fluctuations were puzzling to all dealing with him, and aroused curiosity in some people and disbelief in others.

## Saeed (20-year-old male)

Saeed is a young man with a diagnosis of autism and learning difficulty. He has not developed any verbal language, and thus no means of expressing his wishes, feelings, likes and dislikes. People like Saeed who live in residential care are at the mercy of the environments, systems, programmes and staff who care for them – all factors beyond their control and all factors which can make or break them. Autistic individuals in this group who are passive and are sensitive may feel overwhelmed and distressed, and become unable to cope. They are unable to complain or ask for things to be done differently, or to tell anyone what is happening to them. In such situations, some autistic individuals who are extrovert may react by showing challenging and antisocial behaviour. However, those in the passive group usually start breaking down with early signs of catatonia. If these are picked up, or if parents are listened to, further breakdown and catatonia can be avoided. Sadly, as in the case of Saeed, I have come across many similar cases where parents' concerns have been ignored and blatantly dismissed, and steps to improve things are not taken until it is too late. Saeed's story is an example of many others who have had similar experiences, and where families have had to fight endless battles, take legal action or remove their son or daughter from residential care and take them home.

Saeed had severe autism and learning difficulty and no verbal language. From a young age, he had shown a tendency to become highly anxious in some settings. He showed extreme sensitivity to noisy and 'busy' surroundings. Saeed showed a severe regression between the ages of two and three years, and had a shutdown episode when he started primary school. He stopped eating for 14 days and had to be hospitalised. Thus, Saeed showed a vulnerability to regression and catatonia-related breakdown when he could not cope with the sensory and demand overload, which caused him anxiety and stress.

During the rest of his school history, Saeed did not have further setbacks and went from strength to strength with the dedicated and combined efforts of his parents and the school in understanding his idiosyncratic sensitivity and needs, and using autism-friendly methods which benefited him. Care was taken not to overload him and to avoid busy and noisy places. He was also taught to indicate a need to leave a situation which he could not cope with.

Saeed was able to learn practical skills and to enjoy a whole range of meaningful activities and had a good quality of life while living at home. He particularly enjoyed swimming, horse riding, hill walking and cycling. He showed a great capacity to be happy, cheerful and enjoy life.

Saeed's breakdown and onset of autistic catatonia started during a residential placement at the age of 19 years. Initially, with careful transition, Saeed seemed to settle well and attended activities with staff support.

However, within about three months after the transition period, Saeed began to deteriorate in his behaviour and ability to cope. Retrospective analysis of staff reports indicated that Saeed had become increasingly anxious and distressed in this placement, and increasingly less able to function and participate in activities. Staff had documented various issues which were classic early signs of autism-related breakdown and catatonia but these were not recognised as such. These included the following:

- refusing to get dressed
- refusing to attend activities
- slowness through morning routine
- getting stuck and 'freezing' episodes
- refusing to eat breakfast
- becoming more repetitive and ritualistic
- behaviours of anger and frustration – chinning, hitting out.

Unfortunately, Saeed's parents' increasing concerns and their knowledge with regard to his anxiety and individual needs and management were not acted upon or implemented with a view to supporting Saeed and reducing his anxiety. From the concerns and detailed documentation, there were very obvious factors in the environment and management which would have been traumatic for Saeed and made him extremely anxious in view of his profile of severe autism and specific needs. One of the most anxiety- and trauma-provoking situations for Saeed would be having to eat in a busy dining room, and being denied food and drink if he did not. Also, once Saeed started breaking down and not coping, he would have found it traumatic to participate in group social events, and his anxiety would have escalated but the signs were not picked up and he was not taken out of the situation. Even when Saeed asked to leave situations, this was refused by the staff. As in other similar cases, this placement did not understand Saeed's severe autism and his complex and individual needs arising from this. This was a placement which was for people with learning disabilities and was not autism specific; however, I have come across a similar lack of understanding in autism-specific placements which are supposed to be specialist in autism.

Saeed's severe anxiety state and the breakdown and the pattern of autism-related catatonia continued to progress after he returned home. This would be the expected pattern as the negative effects of the trauma, distress and anxiety would have long-lasting impact in a similar way to that seen in people suffering from post-traumatic stress disorder. Saeed was frightened to leave the house or to change out of his pyjamas. He lashed out if his parents insisted on him getting dressed, and went into a state of panic if they tried to get him in the car or take him on a short walk. The freezing episodes and movement difficulties with crossing thresholds continued and escalated with Saeed 'getting stuck' and unable to get up from the toilet for up to seven hours on some occasions. The management of the catatonia with intensive one-to-one support and a structured individual programme with very gradual and planned extensions reduced the frequency and duration of the freezing episodes.

Saeed continued to show the following pattern of catatonia and related breakdown which affected the quality of his life and that of his parents in ways which most people would not be able to imagine.

Saeed's parents will never risk residential care again, and have the huge burden of caring for Saeed at home.

## Catatonia behaviours manifested in Saeed

- freezing and getting stuck at transitions and thresholds, for example, freezing at the bottom of the stairs, pulling trousers part way up, getting in and out of the car

- movement difficulties, for example, clenched hands, rocking, hands jammed in pockets, episodes of involuntary shaking and tremor

- odd movements and postures, for example, crouching, fixed eye gaze while twisting his head over his shoulder

- difficulty making choices or decisions

- increase in rituals and repetitive behaviours, for example, wanting to change trousers repeatedly, asking for pyjamas, verbally repetitive, repeatedly doing the same few jigsaws, and sometimes dismantling and assembling them repeatedly

- slowness in movements and routines on some days

- needing prompts to complete actions and to engage in activities

- eating and drinking difficulties on some days

- difficulty passing urine regularly (which was likely to be due to the catatonia, but it was important to rule out other causes).

## Other difficulties related to autism breakdown

Saeed showed various other behaviours characteristic of autism breakdown. He showed less resilience and a lower threshold to becoming anxious. He showed an increase in rituals and repetitive behaviours, for example, wanting to change his trousers repeatedly and wanting keys in locks. He insisted on doing things in set ways. He showed less focus, concentration, motivation, engagement and enjoyment. He became hyper-aroused when left to his own devices and had periods of agitation and increased tendency to show behaviours such as hitting out and hitting on his chin.

## Gayle (29-year-old female)

Gayle lives in New Zealand. She contacted me in desperation for confirmation of her diagnosis of catatonia which she knew applied to her. I am including her story in here as it illustrates how catatonia can intermittently cause temporary shutdown and other debilitating phenomena in autistic people who are able to function really well at other times. They are able to study at university and be in employment provided they get recognition and support for the catatonic episodes. Gayle also exemplifies many high functioning individuals in the UK and worldwide who contact me with similar stories and are desperately trying to get relevant help and support. Some of these people have lived and struggled with the episodic and intermittent catatonia-type difficulties all their life, and are only realising recently that their difficulties have been due to catatonia.

An assessment based on a Skype interview with Gayle and her support workers and descriptions contained in the reports of other professionals who had assessed Gayle confirmed the following picture of her difficulties related to catatonia:

- Gayle had experienced episodes of 'freezing' since high school and these had become increasingly worse.

- Gayle sometimes became 'frozen' or 'stuck' and was then unable to complete movements and actions without external prompts from another person. This did not occur all the time, but in certain situations and on certain days. On some days, Gayle was unable to make herself move in the mornings and was unable to get out of bed. Her support workers reported that they needed to give her verbal and physical prompts to enable her to move.

- Gayle experienced more freezing and 'getting stuck' episodes when she was on her own. Gayle described an incident when she was in the middle of a shower and was suddenly unable to make any movement in order to initiate the action of turning off the shower, and was unable to speak to call out for help.

When the support workers were with her, they provided physical external support by holding her hand and giving her prompts. This enabled Gayle to keep moving and not become 'stuck'. In the mornings, Gayle had help from support workers who prompt her. Otherwise she would not be able to get ready or leave the room to go to college.

- In certain situations, Gayle was unable to talk and became totally mute. Her support worker reported that on one occasion, Gayle went mute for over an hour. During these episodes, Gayle felt as if her vocal cords were stuck and she was unable to speak. In general, Gayle struggled to communicate verbally due to these difficulties and preferred to communicate by writing.

- Gayle also experienced difficulties in chewing and swallowing at times. On occasions Gayle was able to raise a glass to her lips but was unable to carry out the action of drinking.

- Gayle was sometimes unable to get up to use the bathroom, and thus had mild incontinence problems.

- Gayle had brief episodes of becoming totally absent and unresponsive suddenly. These had been noticed by her support workers (mental freezing and shutdown).

- Gayle showed lots of hesitations and pauses during motor activity which had been observed by the occupational therapist.

- A psychologist who had assessed Gayle had noted her freezing and shutdown as unusual behaviours as follows:

    In session there have been instances when Gayle appears to 'freeze in position' and behaves in an unusual manner. Her responses at these times will completely freeze, she does not respond to any instructions or communication, she maintains a fixed eye gaze and there is absence of any verbal communication. On one particular occasion in session, she engaged in this behaviour towards the end of the session and continued to engage in this behaviour for 40 minutes…

- Gayle also showed other involuntary catatonia behaviours such as jerks of the entire body, eye rolling, repetitive blinking and snorting.

Gayle carries on stoically with pursuing her life goals and bravely fights and overcomes each hurdle that comes her way. Her life has been made a bit easier with the diagnosis of catatonia in terms of others understanding her and providing her the right kind of support and funding. However, the problems and the struggle continue but she does not give up, and her courage is truly admirable.

## Kevin (23-year-old male)

Kevin is a young man in his 20s on the autistic spectrum with extremely high intelligence (with some cognitive abilities in the gifted range). He has the most gentle, kind, friendly and endearing personality. His ambition is to work in the computer gaming industry to which his intelligence, special skills and interest would be extremely well suited.

Despite his high intelligence and capability, Kevin has underachieved, both academically and in his independence and social development. Although Kevin likes people and is extremely friendly, kind and empathetic, his social interaction and social life have been affected severely by his passivity and debilitating autism stress and anxiety. Kevin has had a tendency to internalise his anxiety and stress and non-coping, and mask his difficulties outside home.

Starting from the age of nine years, Kevin's symptoms of anxiety and non-coping have been diagnosed as his traits of Asperger syndrome and obsessive compulsive disorder (OCD). From age nine he has been treated with a variety of psychiatric medications and psychological therapies including cognitive behaviour therapy, solution focused therapy and family therapy. Kevin did not improve but continued to deteriorate. None of the professionals involved recognised Kevin's long-standing features of catatonia and the subsequent severe catatonia and autism breakdown. The professionals concerned did not link the severity of his catatonia to the psychiatric medications. Kevin now shows a complex pattern of autism-related breakdown which includes complex catatonia at a physical and mental level and overlap with compulsive thoughts and behaviours.

Kevin's manifestation of catatonia and related breakdown is described below.

## Catatonia features

Kevin has shown various catatonia features from childhood including the following:

- holding his hands in peculiar and unusual postures
- repeated approach and withdrawal when picking up an object
- hesitation and repetition when walking, especially through doorways
- repetitive arm movements
- complex automatic motor movements as if in a trance – being on his tiptoes, moving backwards and forwards and waving his arms in repetitive movements.

## Catatonia-type breakdown

Kevin has shown the complex manifestations which occur in high functioning autistic people in the following ways.

### Freezing and being stuck

Kevin becomes stuck in ritual and repetitive routines. During these rituals, Kevin also experiences thought repetition and becoming stuck in a loop of repetitive or rigid thought pattern which he cannot get out of. The thoughts can be anything like 'I've said the wrong thing' or 'something bad will happen if I don't do this'. When Kevin becomes stuck in these repetitive thoughts, they are overwhelming and all consuming. He cannot get out of them himself and needs someone else to break the cycle for him.

### Episodes of shutdown catatonia state

These more severe episodes started occurring after Kevin was treated with quetiapine, and increased in frequency, duration and severity.

The following quote from notes written by Kevin's parents describes what happens during these episodes of shutdown.

an increase in repetitive movements and hesitations; difficulty crossing thresholds, using stairs, sitting down, getting out of bed, etc.;

Reduced speech including complete mutism;

Pushing food out of his mouth with his tongue (automatically);

Unable to carry out everyday tasks, including dressing, washing, cleaning teeth, eating, using the toilet, etc.;

Huge increase in getting stuck.

At times, Kevin is unable to sit upright or hold himself, and his head becomes stooped or he sprawls over the table with his head down. Kevin also finds it difficult to chew and swallow at these times (due to movement difficulties of catatonia).

At these times, all of the above daily functions have to be carried out by his parents, including physically prompting and assisting him with everything. They have to physically get him off the settee, take him up the stairs, take him to the toilet, wash him, dress him and feed him.

When Kevin is out of these episodes, he is able to describe how he feels during them. In response to my questions, he gave the following description of feeling extreme anxiety and panic and of feeling trapped.

> When it starts to get bad, I can feel it getting worse…feel more anxious…feel a lot of tension in my body…can feel a little unwell, sick, nauseous, very panicky, mixture of stress and very high anxiety… Feel trying to do anything is all too much, can't relax, want to get up and move but feel trapped, I can't do that. When I try and move, when it is that bad, I feel I shouldn't have done it, or done it in the wrong way.

## Situational variability in catatonia

Kevin shows extreme situational variability in his functioning. When he was younger, his behaviour and functioning were very different between home and school. His teachers never saw the extreme anxiety and manifestations of breakdown which he showed at home. In adulthood, he shows the same extreme patterns. He has the worst episodes of catatonia and related difficulties at home. When he is outdoors either with his family or with other people (including professionals assessing him), he is able to mask/overcome his difficulties and is fluid in his movements, speech and thought processes.

I saw this aspect first hand in Kevin when I assessed him on two separate occasions. The first time, he had been in good form without being in a catatonia shutdown episode. He was most polite and friendly, and seemed very pleased to see me. He did not show any outward signs of being anxious or stressed. He seemed relaxed and his movements on that day were fluid without any hesitations, but he did show a tendency of some repetitive movements of his arms and legs. He was able to walk through doorways and in the garden in a very relaxed manner, and related to me with ease and a friendly manner.

Before my next visit, his parents informed me that Kevin had gone into the shutdown catatonia state described above. I decided to see him anyway.

When I arrived, Kevin looked pale and seemed distant and barely spoke in a whisper. I told him that I wanted to carry out a psychometric test with him and he agreed. Gradually, he became more alert, more communicative and engaged fully with the tasks, both verbal and non-verbal. In fact, as we did the tests, he was back to as I had seen him previously. He made eye contact, spoke in his normal tone of voice and concentrated fully on each task. On timed tasks, he was aware of the need to work fast and tried his best.

His parents feel that after Kevin has been in situations where he has managed to function 'normally', his difficulties related to catatonia and compulsions are even more severe after he arrives home. During a visit abroad with his family for an extended family reunion, Kevin was described as 'back to his normal self' and enjoying every minute in a relaxed and carefree way. Yet, within minutes of arriving back home, he slipped back into his catatonia and loop of becoming stuck in repetitive thoughts and compulsions and was unable to carry out voluntary activities although he wanted to. Kevin's contrast in functioning between home and outside home epitomises one of the most enigmatic aspects of autism-related catatonia which is baffling, frustrating and stressful both for the individual and those who love and care for them. Yet, on the positive side, people like Kevin at least have good days when they are able to enjoy life and be out of the loop of repetitive thoughts and fears and free from the paralytic chains of the catatonia even if it is for a temporary period.

## Ongoing difficulties

Kevin and his family are currently struggling with the aftermath and severe withdrawal symptoms of antidepressant medication which he has been having very long term as prescribed treatment. They are victims of not being made aware about the addictive risks of long-term psychiatric medications and professional dismissal about their concerns and requests for help to enable him to withdraw from these medications. The irony of the sad situation is that the psychiatric medications were clearly not helping and no one could see the damage they were causing. To add insult to injury, Kevin is now experiencing horrendous withdrawal symptoms which are not being recognised as such by the medical professionals involved. The All Party Parliamentary Group for Prescribed Drug Dependence is currently aiming for families to get support and medical practitioners to get better training so that such disasters capable of ruining people's lives are avoided. However, it will take time for mission statements to translate to change and support for individuals and families, and this is a little too late for Kevin and his family. For Kevin, the future is uncertain and it remains to be seen whether his ambition of working in the computer industry or with animals remains a pipe dream or will be achieved. Knowing Kevin and his amazing, courageous and supportive family behind him, I feel optimistic that he will make it. He has to… (no pressure, Kevin!).

## Rita (25-year-old female)

Rita's story is representative of young highly intelligent people at university who develop debilitating 'freezing' and 'mutism' episodes and may not have had the diagnosis of autism.

Rita was an academic high flyer with extremely high standards for herself in terms of academic achievement and social participation. She had developed 'cognitive' and 'intellectual' strategies for coping in social situations at school and university, and learnt about relationships from television and films. She had a mental health breakdown with marked features of catatonia of the type which occurs in people who are intellectually high functioning. Rita's manifestation of catatonia started gradually with increased slowness in communication. Over time, she developed intermittent episodes of freezing, mutism and being stuck in bed or on the floor for hours. Rita and her family made the connection of her symptoms to autism-related catatonia, and pursed a diagnosis of autism and catatonia.

People like Rita who have supportive families are able to research their symptoms and pursue a diagnostic clarification of their autism and catatonia. However, there are likely to be many more young people at university who are having similar difficulties who may not have the support, resources or motivation to seek help.

The following extract from an email from a young person at university exemplifies the situation:

> I'm getting in touch as I believe I have autistic catatonia and would like to explore options for diagnosis (it's proving extremely debilitating, but the condition isn't recognised by professionals at the local mental health service). I have freezes (normally between ten minutes and an hour) around five times a day, and have also had problems with selective mutism, which would last up to ten waking hours, but has become much less frequent since freezes became more frequent. In addition to the catatonic symptoms, I show clear signs of autism, and my friends and I suspected I had autism long before the catatonia symptoms began. If you have any idea on how I might get diagnosed (if there is anyone able to diagnose in the north/within the NHS), it would be very helpful, I would be really grateful. Regardless, thank you so much for your research into this condition.

# Chapter 4

# Consequences of Misdiagnosis and Misconception

## Difficulties faced by parents and individuals when seeing professionals

Many professionals do not understand the complex manifestations of chronic catatonia in people with ASD. Professionals may recognise and diagnose acute, severe catatonia in ASD in its most severe form as described above. However, in the majority of people with ASD, the complex manifestations of chronic catatonia are not recognised or diagnosed by professionals who are consulted by desperate families when the person with ASD shows complex patterns of deterioration and difficulties in addition to their underlying autism. I have been contacted by families, carers, care staff, teachers and high functioning individuals themselves who have experienced the following from health professionals:

- disbelief
- lack of knowledge and understanding about autism-related catatonia and related breakdown
- unwillingness to learn or be informed
- being passed around professionals in different disciplines
- lack of support and empathy
- inability to appreciate the seriousness of the condition
- wrong assumption that the person with catatonia is 'faking' it and that they can control it

- inability to appreciate that chronic catatonia can deteriorate to severe levels

- being told that the behaviours of concern are part of the person's autism and nothing to worry about

- unwillingness to review/withdraw psychiatric medication which could be triggering and contributing to the catatonia

- refusal to support referral for a specialist assessment/opinion

- being told that it was not necessary to add another label to the person's diagnosis of autism and would not be helpful

- parents heavily criticised and also being subjected to risk assessments, for example if the young person is not able to attend school

- being told that 'catatonia' is an ancient concept and no longer exists.

I get contacted by desperate parents all the time. The following extract from an email sent to me recently is similar to many others and epitomises what the parents have to face and endure:

> We are contacting you in desperation and hope that you can help us. Until approximately three years ago, X had been a happy and placid child despite his autism. However, in recent years there has been a marked change in his behaviour and wellbeing. We contacted our GP who referred us to a mental health team. This led to further referrals and assessments but without any progress or conclusions. X's difficulties in behaviour and movement with freezing episodes continue to worsen and we had no idea what was happening until the headmistress at his school mentioned the possibility of autistic catatonia. This was the first time we had heard of this condition. We were hoping for a diagnosis of autistic catatonia when we met with the NHS psychiatrist yesterday after a long wait. The psychiatrist tested for signs of catatonia by lifting our son's arm in various positions, and concluded that he was not showing catatonia and it was probably depression, and prescribed antidepressants. She was not interested in hearing or reading about autism-related catatonia and dismissed us without any concern about the seriousness of the situation or our stress and worry.

## Misdiagnosis and the implications

It is worrying when the catatonia in people with autism is not recognised or diagnosed in the early manifestations before it escalates and reaches severe levels of disability and difficulty. It is even more worrying and of concern that many people who present with catatonia or catatonia-type deterioration are misdiagnosed and given a variety of diagnoses. In our clinical and research work over the years, we have come across a variety of diagnoses or explanations given by professionals to explain the deterioration and symptoms in autistic people who have developed catatonia of varying levels. The range of diagnoses and explanations have included schizophrenia, depression, manic depression, obsessive compulsive disorder, epilepsy, challenging behaviour, adult autism, 'part of their autism', wilfulness, laziness, stubbornness and malingering.

Such misconception and misdiagnosis has severe implications for the individual and their family. The stories below of some autistic people in whom the catatonia has not been recognised at an early stage or been misconceived or misdiagnosed illustrate this.

## The story of Max

Max is a young man who had a catatonia-type breakdown during his final year at university which was not diagnosed as such. Max had been highly intelligent and a high achiever at school and did not have any diagnosis when he followed his ambition and went to university. Unfortunately, Max was unable to cope with the social demands and pressures of university, and started having difficulties during his second year. These difficulties were mild at first although in retrospect it became clear that they resembled catatonia-type deterioration affecting his speech, eating, passivity and level of activity. He improved when he was home during the summer vacation. His deterioration continued after he returned to university for the final year, and Max was unable to continue at university and was brought home by his parents. Max was admitted to a psychiatric hospital and initially treated as having an acute psychotic episode.

At the time of his breakdown, Max did not have a diagnosis of an ASD or Asperger syndrome; in fact, it was four years after his initial breakdown that Max had the diagnosis of Asperger syndrome and catatonia from an external professional. During those four years, Max was under the mental health team and was given various psychiatric diagnoses including 'psychotic illness' and depression, and was treated with various psychiatric medications. The external consultant psychiatrist who made the diagnosis of Asperger syndrome and catatonia pointed out in his report that in his view Max had never shown any definite psychotic symptoms or a clear history of depressive illness. However, this was ignored by the psychiatrists treating Max.

Max had also reacted very badly to one of the drugs (citalopram). He was described as being in a 'coma' for ten days. He became unresponsive and stopped eating and drinking. The description sounds like an episode of acute, severe catatonia triggered by the side effects of the drug. This indicated that Max was extremely vulnerable to the side effects of such drugs, but this was not recognised or taken into account and Max continued to be treated with psychiatric medication. Max's catatonia continued to worsen and he also started showing bizarre, uncharacteristic behaviours. The medical professionals failed to recognise these as possible adverse side effects of the medication, and seemed oblivious of the diagnosis of Asperger syndrome and catatonia which had been confirmed by several external professionals. His various fluctuating symptoms and behaviours kept on being interpreted as psychotic symptoms and/or negative and positive symptoms of schizophrenia. This is not unusual and I have noted frequently that clinicians inexperienced in assessing people with Asperger syndrome and catatonia often continue to misinterpret behaviours, vocalisations and clinical presentation as psychotic or schizophrenic phenomena. When the person with catatonia is treated with psychiatric medication, this can lead to all sorts of disturbances in the mental state. Like Max, the person can show complex manifestations of the condition ranging from immobility and stupor to a whole range of abnormalities of movement and behaviour, including excitement, euphoria, irrelevant and repetitive speech and rituals. People with catatonia can also experience a range of odd bodily, perceptual and sensory phenomena.

In Max's case, it would have been most helpful if all professionals concerned in his case had accepted and understood Max's diagnosis of Asperger syndrome and catatonia and focused on the management of these aspects. Instead they continued the search for alternative or other co-morbid diagnostic labels for explaining Max's symptoms and behaviour phenomena. Other psychiatric diagnoses such as psychosis, schizophrenia and depression were misleading and led to medication trials which exacerbated and complicated Max's catatonia and its manifestation.

Besides the medication trials, at one point Max was also detained in a psychiatric hospital located 200 miles from his home. The stress suffered by Max and his family during this period is unimaginable. It was only his parents' courage, determination and relentless care and support which eventually enabled Max to be 'rescued' from the web of the psychiatric system. Max's parents gave up on the 'services' and enabled Max to recover and regain some of his skills by their dedicated care and application of the psycho-ecological approach described in this book.

There are long-term (probably lifelong) implications for Max of the misdiagnosis and inappropriate medical treatments. Although he has recovered from the catatonia aspects and he is happier, he has not totally regained his skills, independence and communication abilities. His family has recently sent me an update:

> Max has been discharged from the mental health services for many years now, and is medication free. All his deranged blood results and weight returned to normal once the psychotropic medications were reduced and stopped. He lives in his own home, has a good quality of life and the GP manages his care. We found your non-medical APT [previous acronym for the psycho-ecological approach] has helped our son in a more sustainable way.

## Jasmine's story

Jasmine lived in a specialist care home for autistic adults. She was referred to me for a clinical psychology assessment and advice regarding 'an increase in ritualistic behaviours', refusing to speak at times, taking a long time to finish meals, refusing to participate in activities, and at times showing uncharacteristic aggressive outbursts.

Jasmine's increase in ritualistic behaviours had been diagnosed as OCD phenomena and psychiatric medication was being used to treat this. Staff in the care home interpreted Jasmine's other difficulties and behaviours as wilfulness, being stubborn and 'attempts to try their patience'. Staff felt that Jasmine had complete control over these behaviours especially as in certain situations she was able to function well and was not slow or 'stubborn'.

When I assessed Jasmine, the misunderstanding and misdiagnosis of her difficulties was all too apparent. Jasmine was in fact showing a breakdown in the form of catatonia, and also extra-pyramidal type side effects of the medication being used to treat her 'OCD' diagnosis. Behaviours which were interpreted as OCD rituals were catatonic phenomena and extra-pyramidal side effects of the medication. Examples are as follows:

- Jasmine was showing the slowness associated with the catatonia, and standing and kneeling in a fixed posture and 'freezing'.

- She was having difficulty in initiating and completing movements and then finishing a movement quickly with a bang or a jerk. What was interpreted as OCD and an increase in rituals was due to Jasmine hesitating, walking to and fro, trying to sit down, getting stuck midway through actions and activities and freezing.

- Jasmine was also showing extra-pyramidal side effects such as tremors, eyes rolling and staring in a fixed gaze.

- Jasmine's slowness and difficulty in eating was due to swallowing and chewing difficulties related to the catatonia. These were interpreted as stubbornness and 'trying their patience'. The more staff pressured her to hurry up, the more stuck she was getting.

- Her 'refusal to 'speak' in some situations was not in her control but due to difficulty in making the movements needed to speak. Similarly, her apparent refusal to join in for activities and outings was due to difficulties in initiating movements and activity related to the catatonia. What was being interpreted as 'refusal' was in fact an inability due to Jasmine having intermittent difficulties with voluntary movements due to the onset of catatonia.

- Jasmine's uncharacteristic outbursts of aggression were also linked to the catatonia as the difficulties related to the catatonia would have caused her a lot of frustration, which she would not be able to express verbally any more.

Jasmine's story illustrates how well-meaning care staff and professionals can misinterpret behaviours leading to a cycle of mismanagement and increased stress for the individual, and a complex pattern of behaviours which become even more difficult to disentangle and interpret. An early recognition of Jasmine's catatonia would have avoided this.

## The story of Shaan

Shaan is a young man in his early 20s who now has a very severe and complex form of catatonia complicated by side effects of various psychiatric medications over the years.

Shaan started showing movement difficulties and abnormalities while he was still at school. These included 'posturing', 'hesitations and freezing', involuntary jerky movements and 'absences'. These were queried as to whether Shaan was having seizure activity but various medical professionals including a paediatrician with a special interest in epilepsy and a consultant child and adolescent psychiatrist concluded that it was not epilepsy but behavioural. Fortunately, due to their insight, Shaan was not started on anti-epileptic medication. Shaan also started having aggressive outbursts and he was unfortunately put on anti-psychotic medication from a young age rather than using a psychological approach to understand and manage all aspects of his behaviour.

Unfortunately, after leaving school Shaan was referred to the Adult Learning Disabilities Service and his involuntary movements such as jerks were interpreted as epileptic seizure activity. He was put on anti-epileptic medication in addition to the anti-psychotic medication. It was not possible to carry out an EEG so the diagnosis of epilepsy was based on staff observations and interpretations of his behaviours. These movement abnormalities were more likely to be associated with the catatonia rather than epilepsy especially in view of the fact that Shaan was showing a very clear picture of a catatonia-type breakdown.

Shaan had shown various aspects of catatonia-like deterioration over the years, which were described by carers but were not recognised as such. The behaviours relating to catatonia were instead misinterpreted as 'psychotic' and 'epileptic':

- Movement difficulties and getting 'stuck' or 'frozen' – Shaan had got stuck in one position for long periods, and had also spent long periods in the toilet at home and at the day centre, and in the bath at the care home. These were interpreted as behaviour difficulties rather than catatonia aspects.

- Movement abnormalities/dystonia – Shaan exhibited these, including sudden jerky movements, involuntary movements, holding his arms in a particular odd posture, crouching, touching the floor, other odd unusual behaviours and repetitions: frowning, grimacing, blank stare, and so on. These were observed and noted but not interpreted as catatonia features.

- Eating and drinking difficulties – Shaan had episodes for several hours over a few days when he had been unable to eat or drink. This was misinterpreted as possible depression (rather than movement difficulties of catatonia causing swallowing and chewing difficulties). Shaan was non-verbal and had no means to express these difficulties.

- 'Challenging behaviour' – Shaan had shown episodes of showing sudden behaviours such as standing up startled and suddenly acting aggressively, especially when coming out of a 'stuck' phase or during a 'stuck' phase. Shaan had shown aggressive/challenging behaviours which are both 'automatic' as part of the catatonia episode, or due to confusion and frustration of his unusual experiences which he could not communicate.

Shaan was also showing various secondary effects of the catatonia-related deterioration which included increased social withdrawal, decreasing ability to tolerate activities enjoyed previously and increased sensitivity. At the time of my involvement, Shaan had a very poor quality of life. He was spending hours stuck in the bath and hours engaging in stereotypic repetitive activities in his bedroom and staff were finding it very difficult to engage him in any activity.

Shaan's management of the catatonia has become very complex due to the increased severity of the difficulties. Early identification and non-medical management would have prevented this level of severity and enabled Shaan to have a much better quality of life despite his severe autism, learning difficulties and severe language impairment. The very sad fact is that Shaan is only in his 20s and has a whole life ahead of him. It remains to be seen how well he can recover from the catatonia-related breakdown and regain his quality of life.

## Jay

Jay is a young man who had a diagnosis of high functioning autism from early childhood. He coped at school although he was described in school reports as being very shy, quiet and passive. Jay was well spoken and articulate. He had an excellent memory for routes, particular events and dates; his special skills and interests included reading timetables and maps and using dictionaries and encyclopaedias to look up information. Jay loved being out and about and enjoyed exploring London, travelling independently on public transport.

Jay's behaviour and functioning started to deteriorate gradually during the third year at college. He started to slow down and needed a lot of prompting to do even basic self-care routines of getting up, washing, brushing, and so on. Jay also gradually spoke less, and finally stopped speaking completely. Total mutism seemed to happen overnight after an incident when he had a panic attack while travelling in a car and needed to get out. A few weeks after this incident, Jay had sudden uncharacteristic outbursts when he suddenly got up, became destructive and smashed things. Jay was admitted to a psychiatric unit for a brief period, and then was placed in full-time care at a residential home for people with learning disabilities. There was some immediate improvement in his mood and behaviour. Jay enjoyed the outings organised by staff and travelling to places of interest in the minibus as he had always enjoyed travelling which he had done independently previously. The staff seemed unaware of his level of intelligence, special skills and interests, and previous ability, independence and communication ability. The slowness, lack of communication, hesitations, repetitive movements and other behaviours related to Jay's breakdown with catatonia were not questioned and the staff's perception and expectation of Jay were a lot lower than he was capable of.

The misdiagnosis of his breakdown as psychotic and behaviour problems and the lack of recognition of the catatonia had severe implications for Jay and his quality of life. As he became slower and started having difficulty with talking, the staff at his residential home began excluding him from outings, which had been the highlights for Jay's existence. He was excluded because he had become so slow in getting ready that he was never ready on time. Also, at times when the staff asked him if he wanted to go on the outing, Jay either took a long time to reply or his hesitation was misinterpreted as a 'no'. At times, Jay became incontinent (due to the difficulty of getting up from his chair to use the toilet); he also showed marked agitation on occasions. These were interpreted as behaviour difficulties and his psychiatric medication was increased.

Jay was treated with a variety of anti-psychotic, antidepressant and anti-epileptic medication. He continued to deteriorate in his self-help skills, independence and abilities and became withdrawn and non-communicative. Jay's family was extremely concerned that Jay was not showing any improvement and in fact continued to deteriorate.

The staff and the various professionals involved with Jay failed to recognise that he was showing autistic catatonia and related breakdown, and that the medication was not helping but making him worse. By the time of my assessment, Jay's catatonia and breakdown had deteriorated to the point where he was unable to get out of bed or a chair, or carry out any voluntary movements or actions without prompts or assistance. Jay also showed a whole range of posture and movement abnormalities. These included stooped posture, stiff movements, dystonia, rocking, body jerks and twitching, grimacing, facial contortions and involuntary smiling, teeth grinding, continuous blinking and repetitive mouth movements. Jay also had difficulty holding his head up or looking up. His whole demeanour was lifeless (apart from the uncontrollable repetitive movements). There was no joy or spark in him. Every little action was a huge effort for him, and there was no way he could communicate his struggle, his imprisonment and his sorrow. The secondary effects included incontinence, loss of skills and independence, an inability to pursue his special interests and a very poor quality of life. Jay was also unable to continue his part-time voluntary office job at a special school. It was distressing and of great concern to his family to witness Jay's gradual and severe deterioration and the negative effects of the psychiatric medications. Fortunately for Jay, they took steps to obtain specialist assessment and advice before it was too late.

## Zoe's experience

Zoe is a girl who has excelled academically and sailed through school and university, but had a breakdown after leaving university. Zoe did not have a diagnosis of autism and coped in social situations with elaborate strategies and rules which she had worked out intellectually and from books, films and her observations of people. She developed mild catatonia symptoms at the age of 23 which gradually increased to a most severe level. Her catatonic episodes were triggered when she interpreted herself breaking a social rule or impinging on someone else. Zoe showed all the classic symptoms of catatonia including mutism, freezing and shutdown episodes. These included episodes when she could not get out of bed or move her limbs or body for hours. Zoe and her family consulted a psychiatrist and asked specifically if she had developed catatonia (which they had deduced from their own research). The psychiatrist dismissed this and told them that catatonia was an ancient concept and did not exist any more. This had a devastating effect on Zoe as it made her feel that she was making it all up, and was causing everyone around her to suffer as a result. She suffered increased guilt and self-blame and started having suicidal thoughts. The family felt that the lack of professional recognition and diagnosis had pushed her to a situation whereby she became a major suicide risk.

Fortunately, Zoe and her family did not give up and found the link between autism and catatonia, which made them pursue the diagnosis of autism and catatonia. Zoe has now been diagnosed with autism and catatonia. This has been a huge relief to her. She is now able to understand a lot about her difficulties in social situations, and her sensory sensitivity issues due to the autism. She has been able to work out the situations which overwhelm her and can lead to shutdown and catatonia episodes. The diagnosis of autism and catatonia and an awareness of the sensory factors which affect her will enable her to develop her own coping strategies, and hopefully avoid shutdown and catatonic episodes.

Zoe's story illustrates how the diagnosis of catatonia can be missed even when someone has such obvious and severe symptoms, and the devastating effect this can have on an individual. Zoe's family persevered with their own research and questioning to find the truth. However, many individuals and families may not have the resources or capacity to question a professional opinion. One cannot help but wonder too whether there are individuals who suffered a worse fate than Zoe and did not live to tell the tale.

Chapter 5

# Possible Causal Factors

We noted in the prevalence study (Wing and Shah 2000) that stressful situations and experiences had been a major precipitating factor in most of the autistic individuals who had developed catatonia-like deterioration. Detailed psychological assessments and formulations of individuals referred to us over the years have highlighted the fact that two main types of factors seem responsible for causing catatonia and related breakdown in autistic individuals:

- psychological distress, anxiety, autistic stress and non-coping
- side effects of psychiatric medications.

Each of these is discussed below as an understanding of these possible causal factors is important for prevention, treatment and management.

## Psychological distress, anxiety, autistic stress and non-coping

I prefer to refer to the stress experienced by autistic individuals as autistic stress as their experience of stress, factors which cause them stress and their reaction to stress are specific to autism and related sensitivity and difficulties. The autistic person's special vulnerability to stress and anxiety is well documented in autobiographical accounts (e.g. Grandin 2006), in family accounts (e.g. Park and Park 2006) and by clinicians and researchers (e.g. Baron, Lipsitt and Goodwin 2006; Groden *et al.* 1994).

Autistic people are extremely vulnerable to becoming anxious, distressed and easily overwhelmed in situations which cause them stress. This vulnerability is due to their underlying autistic characteristics, which include social and communication difficulties, sensory sensitivity and cognitive style of focusing on the detail rather than the whole. Due to these characteristics, they often experience the world around them as invasive, chaotic, overwhelming and unpredictable. The psychological distress and autistic stress experienced by autistic individuals often relates to fear, social and general anxiety, demand overload, frustration, fatigue, confusion, misunderstanding and misinterpreting and non-coping. It is not unusual for autistic individuals (children and adults) to react by showing agitation or a behaviour outburst (meltdowns) in situations which they find overwhelming and difficult to cope with. Some autistic individuals (especially those who have a passive personality) may not show an overt outburst or meltdown but may react by withdrawing into themselves, becoming less communicative and responsive and shutting down.

In autistic people, the accumulated effect of distress, autistic stress, anxiety, non-coping and trauma can lead to many types of breakdown. The breakdown can be manifested in different ways, depending on the individual's underlying personality and vulnerability. Some autistic people may react by showing a breakdown in behaviour which presents as challenging behaviours such as physical aggression or self-injurious behaviours. Others may show mental health type breakdown in the form of having psychotic episodes, paranoia, low mood/depression, and so on. Catatonia is one type of breakdown which occurs in autistic individuals and can be manifested in many different ways, as discussed in Chapters 1 and 2.

The factors which cause psychological distress and non-coping to autistic people and can lead to a breakdown in the form of catatonia are related to their underlying autistic sensitivities and needs, and also an inability to express their distress and self-regulate their emotions and reactions. Autistic people (even those who are high functioning) are generally unable to express feelings of anxiety and psychological and emotional distress, and to ask for help and support appropriately. Autistic individuals often feel intense emotion but are unable to express it appropriately. Those who are 'passive' and have initiation difficulties are extremely vulnerable to being exploited, and would be unable to protect themselves, complain or communicate their distress or fears directly. In fact, autistic individuals in the 'passive' group were significantly more likely to develop catatonia-type deterioration compared to other groups on the Wing and Gould (1979) categories of social impairment (Wing and Shah 2000). This has been corroborated by subsequent clinical assessments. In many individuals who become more passive and prompt dependent, the breakdown seems to exacerbate the underlying passivity. The stories in Chapter 3 described the different types of autistic stress, trauma and non-coping which led to the catatonia and related breakdown in the individuals. Many of the stories illustrate a variety of causes of psychological/emotional distress which seems to break the autistic person from within and lead to shutdown, catatonia and a related pattern of breakdown.

To understand factors causing autistic stress, psychological distress and non-coping related to catatonia and breakdown requires an individual approach and a detailed assessment of how the person is affected by the autism, what their sensitivities and needs are at any given stage of life, and an analysis of what they are having to cope with. This is explained in more detail in Chapter 7.

There is often not a single cause which can account for the catatonia and related breakdown. Sometimes, there may be multiple causes or cumulative effect of various factors. It is also not always possible to identify the exact potential causes, but only to make the best assumption possible based on the individual's profile of autism, their sensitivity and how this matches with their environment, demands and lifestyle.

The following sections highlight some possible causal factors identified in individuals assessed by the author.

## Ecological/milieu factors

- being in environments, programmes or services inappropriate to their autistic needs

- lack of daily structure, routine and occupation appropriate to their ability and autism

- lack of an appropriate type and level of stimulation

- being in settings which are too demanding, for example being in mainstream school, college or university without adequate support

- trying to cope with independence beyond their capability (for example, living away from home)

- inappropriate peer group and social media pressure
- environments and situations which cause sensory and autistic overload (for example, noise, chaos, lack of structure).

## Psychological factors

- sensory overload – specific triggers or generally being overwhelmed
- emotional overload – many autistic people feel positive and negative emotions very strongly to the point of becoming overwhelmed
- negative social experiences such as bullying, abuse, violence and exploitation
- negative 'institutional' experiences described by some autistic people as feeling 'crushed'
- lack of diagnosis of autism (especially in high functioning people)
- feelings of pressure, guilt and underachievement – in very intellectually high functioning girls especially
- not coping when the normal 'cognitive' and 'logical' strategies do not work in novel or unexpected social situations/ relationships. This affects high functioning individuals (especially girls) who have been able to get by without a diagnosis of autism by 'masking' their difficulties with cognitive strategies.

## Family/relationship issues

- bereavement
- loss (due to siblings leaving home, divorce, etc.)
- change in family composition (for example, birth of a sibling, half-siblings moving in)
- coping with closeness and intimacy.

## Adverse effects of psychiatric medications/ drug-induced catatonia

It is now recognised that many psychiatric medications can cause catatonia or catatonia-like conditions (Dhossche, Shah and Wing 2006a; Fink and Taylor 2003). There is a huge overlap between catatonia features and the well-recognised extra-pyramidal and parkinsonian-type side effects of psychiatric medication.

As discussed in Chapter 2, autistic people often have a predisposition to catatonia-related features, which can be present with or without additional breakdown. Many autistic people have a heightened sensitivity to the side effects of medication. It is not surprising then that in some autistic individuals, the psychiatric medications can lead to catatonia and related breakdown.

The advice of psychiatrists experienced in catatonia (Dhossche *et al.* 2006b; Fink, Taylor and Ghaziuddin 2006) is that in any individual who develops catatonia, it is most important to identify any possible culprit psychiatric medication which could be causing the catatonia or contributing to it by making it more severe. If the individual is on any medication which could cause extra-pyramidal and parkinsonian-type side effects, it is crucial for the professionals concerned to withdraw the medication following appropriate guidelines and monitoring. If medication is considered necessary, it would be advisable to select alternative drugs without such side effects for short-term trials and monitor the effects very carefully.

Many autistic people are put on psychiatric medication either due to a misdiagnosis of their symptoms as psychotic, or to treat challenging behaviour and behaviour abnormalities such as repetitive behaviours and obsessions. Sometimes, individuals who present with catatonia and related breakdown are misdiagnosed and inappropriately treated with psychiatric medications such as anti-psychotics, which are likely to exacerbate their breakdown and cause more severe forms of catatonia.

In my clinical experience, psychiatric medication is used too readily (sometimes due to parental demand) for almost any presenting symptom in autistic people and people with learning disability. Unfortunately, it is very rare to see good practice in the use of psychiatric medication for autistic individuals. More often than not, there is a lack of clear rationale, baseline measures, monitoring of effects and caution about side effects. Moreover, instead of short-term trials of a single medication, it is more common to see long-term use of a combination of psychiatric medications. Also, there is very little awareness and consideration of possible addictive and withdrawal effects of these medications on autistic individuals.

It is not unusual to find that autistic individuals, especially those with severe learning disabilities, are on a regime of a cocktail of psychiatric medications. I recently assessed a man of 43 years of age with severe autism and learning disability to advise on the management of his challenging behaviour. I was shocked and flabbergasted to find that this man was on a regime of the following psychiatric medications: two types of anti-psychotic medication; two types of anti-convulsant medication (for behaviour management as he was not epileptic); one antidepressant medication; one benzodiazepine. On top of this, he was prescribed an additional anti-psychotic and another benzodiazepine as required, which were being used by the nursing staff almost daily to manage his agitation.

There is now increasing awareness of the overmedication using psychiatric drugs for people with learning disabilities and/or autism. There is currently a campaign with the acronym 'STOMP' which stands for 'Stopping overmedication of people with learning disabilities'. STOMP was launched in 2016 by:

- NHS England
- the Royal College of Nursing
- the Royal College of GPs
- the Royal Pharmaceutical Society
- the British Psychological Society.

These organisations pledged to work together to stop the overmedication of people with a learning disability, autism or both. Information about the STOMP campaign can be found on the NHS England website.[1]

The campaign is a commitment to reducing the use of medication prescribed with the aim of reducing challenging behaviour and it acknowledges the prioritisation of psychological and other interventions. This may be a little too late for some individuals but

---

1    www.england.nhs.uk/learning-disabilities/improving-health/stomp

hopefully the campaign will have some positive effect on medical professionals' current and future thinking with regard to the use of psychiatric medication for people with learning disabilities and/or autism.

One of the most important requirements of using powerful psychiatric medications which affect brain processes is that the person taking medication should *immediately* report severe side effects. These are usually subjective experiences which would not be apparent externally to others and include effects such as feelings of increased anxiety, agitation, panic, nervousness, dizziness, restlessness and headaches.

Most autistic people (including those with catatonia and breakdown) would not be able to report these effects, for several reasons:

- Most autistic people, even those who have the verbal capacity, have difficulty expressing emotions and internal feelings such as anxiety, agitation, and so on.

- Many autistic individuals are non-verbal and thus do not have the verbal capacity to understand or report any side effects, even if these are experienced severely and are not tolerable.

- One of the most common characteristics of catatonia and related breakdown is reduced speech and ability to communicate. Thus, even the most high functioning individuals who may have been verbal and communicative prior to the breakdown would not have the capacity to report any side effects of medications being given to them during the breakdown.

Autistic individuals who are not able to communicate side effects and feeling of increased anxiety, agitation, panic, sensory distortions, headaches, and so on are likely to show increased behavioural or mental disturbance or even exacerbation of their breakdown. Unfortunately, higher doses of the medication or additional medications are used to try to 'treat' the increased agitation and outbursts, or the increased catatonia symptoms. This often becomes a vicious cycle. In some people who have developed catatonia and related breakdown, the clinical picture becomes so complicated and it is difficult to separate out the drug-induced catatonia elements from the other aspects. Also, there can be significant withdrawal effects when medication is being withdrawn which adds to the vicious cycle, as withdrawal symptoms are often taken as a reason to continue or increase the medications! There is a recent review commissioned by the All Party Parliamentary Group for Prescribed Drug Dependence. The review concluded that withdrawal from antidepressants often causes severe, debilitating symptoms which can last for weeks, months or longer (Davies and Read 2018). In my experience, many medical professionals tend to dismiss the possible effects of psychiatric drug withdrawal in autistic individuals. Families have a very difficult time trying to get professional support and advice when they suspect that the deterioration of symptoms in their son or daughter is due to the effects of drug withdrawal.

## Individual stories illustrating possible causes
### Alice
Alice's story illustrates the detrimental effects of living in a noisy, busy and chaotic environment which is a common cause for breakdown in autistic people who have various sensory sensitivities.

Alice had shown mild features of catatonia for a few years, but these were not affecting her functioning or quality of life. However, she had a catatonia-related breakdown in her 30s which led to problems with walking, 'getting stuck' and episodes of freezing lasting hours. This deterioration affected Alice's quality of life as she could no longer attend day-care, and was often housebound as she was unable to walk and go outdoors.

The detailed psycho-ecological assessment indicated that Alice's deterioration and catatonia-related breakdown were due to autistic stress, psychological distress and possible trauma caused by being in an environment which she was unable to cope with. Alice was living in a residential placement which was supposed to be specialist in autism, but unfortunately the environment and set up were not autism-friendly for someone of Alice's needs. Alice was in an environment which was noisy, chaotic and unstructured. It was one of those units where the television was kept on loud volume throughout the day, sometimes with the radio on at the same time. Alice also witnessed severe challenging behaviour in another resident and was a victim of aggressive outbursts by this resident. Alice became anxious, fearful and traumatised. Her difficulties could be understood as a breakdown in the form of catatonia due to being in situations and environments which had caused her distress and fear and trauma. Alice had not been able to express her distress and fear during the time that her living environment was crowded, noisy and unsafe.

## Zara

Zara's story illustrates the combined negative effects of ecological factors, psychiatric medication and lack of early diagnosis of breakdown and catatonia.

Zara was an autistic girl who was sensitive and became anxious and overwhelmed easily since early childhood. She was happiest when doing activities outdoors such as walking, swimming and trampolining. She loved the feel of air on her face, nature, animals and spacious surroundings. Zara had a breakdown of behaviour when she was nine and started having temper outbursts and engaging in self-injurious behaviours. She was treated with anti-psychotic medication. The self-injurious behaviour reduced, but Zara began to show early signs of catatonia which were not recognised as such. Unfortunately, an antidepressant medication was added. Zara continued to deteriorate and developed a whole range of movement difficulties and abnormalities related to autistic catatonia and had increasing periods of shutdown. She also developed swallowing and chewing difficulties, lost her sparkle and lost a lot of weight.

In Zara's case, the initial behaviour breakdown was related to being in an Applied Behaviour Analysis (ABA) programme, which required her to be in a small room for several hours with intensive one-to-one support. This would be a nightmare scenario and distressing for someone like Zara given her preferences and sensitivities. Zara would not have been able to communicate her distress and frustration and thus had a behaviour breakdown. The anti-psychotic medication used to treat the challenging behaviour seemed to have triggered off the catatonia and related breakdown which gradually worsened as more medication was added and she continued to attend the intensive programme.

## Ricky

Ricky's story exemplifies the occurrence of catatonia and related breakdown in young adults after leaving school. This seems related to the loss of structure, routine and stimulation, and not having an appropriate programme of further education or occupation suitable to their level of intelligence and ability. It seems that without the external structure and routine, and an external programme of activities to follow, these individuals who are usually in the 'passive' subgroup do not have the self-motivation to occupy themselves, or to structure their time and develop constructive routines. Gradually, their behaviour and functioning deteriorate and they develop either a general breakdown or catatonia-related breakdown.

Ricky was a young man with high functioning autism who obtained several GCSEs and coped at a mainstream school. He was fully independent and enjoyed travelling on public transport to places of interest. After leaving school, Ricky tried to attend courses in a college for further education. He did not enjoy these and gradually gave up and stayed at home without any constructive occupation.

Over the course of two years Ricky deteriorated in his functioning, developed various ritualistic behaviours and lost interest in activities and outings he had enjoyed previously. He was treated with antidepressant and anti-psychotic medication which seemed to have no visible effects. Ricky continued to deteriorate and developed catatonia together with a more general breakdown.

## Lou

Lou's story is typical of some young people who are in mainstream school without a diagnosis of autism. The distress, trauma and anxiety generated by coping in a mainstream environment with the social demands, instances of bullying and an inability to express their difficulties leads to shutdown and catatonia-related breakdown. In many of these individuals, the diagnosis of autism is made after the breakdown.

Lou is a highly intelligent girl (with measured intelligence in the gifted range) who was diagnosed with autistic spectrum disorder at the age of 11 years after developing increasing levels of anxiety and social withdrawal at school. Unfortunately, Lou's difficulties were not recognised as autistic catatonia, and they continued at school until she had a total breakdown and was unable to attend. The causal factors related to her underlying autism characteristics and sensitivity and increased demands at secondary school. Lou had an extreme sensitivity to sensory and social aspects of the environment. These aspects included noise, lights, transitions, new environments, busy environments, excessive stimuli and social demands. Lou had also suffered trauma in the past with respect to being bullied and also experiencing too many demands in school at times when her tolerance was low, and she was not able to function or cope well. The final crunch came when Lou moved to secondary school. The transition and the external demands such as rules, new routines and environments and changing classrooms decreased her tolerance further and she developed heightened sensitivity to all sensory aspects. The school did not understand her difficulties and no adjustments were made for Lou's difficulties. Lou was expected and 'forced' to be in environments and situations in which she could not cope. Lou began withdrawing from her environment, demands and interactions and developed increasing periods of shutdown, catatonia and a general breakdown. Lou showed these difficulties by 'freezing', becoming mute and being unable to move or carry out any voluntary activity and 'shutting down'. Lou could interact and communicate and function well for short periods. She would then become exhausted and overwhelmed from the stimulation and the effort involved. At this point, she needed to shut down or only engage in motor stereotypic behaviours such as pacing, bouncing, rocking, flapping, tapping and gesturing repetitively. Lou became unable to attend school, and gradually had fewer and shorter periods when she could function well. She also developed an odd walking gait and developed a stress fracture on her foot due to the extensive pacing and bouncing.

## Jayden

Jayden's story is typical of young autistic people who are unable to cope with the social demands and independence at mainstream college.

Jayden's deterioration in functioning and the onset of catatonia started after he left mainstream school and started attending a further education college for science. Jayden may have been able to cope with the academic demands of the course, but in view of his type of autism, he would have found it very difficult to cope with the social demands and the level of independence required without the structure and support which he would have had at the school. Jayden's inability to cope with the demands and inability to communicate this and ask for help and support led to a regression of his autism and a breakdown in the form of catatonia.

## Ruby

Ruby's story provides an example of a case in which difficulties coping with relationships and experiences of exploitation and abuse had led to ongoing anxiety and intermittent/episodic catatonia.

I have been contacted by various high functioning women with autism who have varying degrees of catatonia-type freezing difficulties. Most of these women have experienced difficulties in social relationships. Many have been exploited in relationships and social situations and suffered various kinds of bullying, abuse and rejections. Sometimes, the pressure of being in a romantic relationship and coping with intimacy is anxiety provoking and stressful. In some, the trauma has led to generalised anxiety disorder and catatonia-related breakdown difficulties on some days. Yet, on other days, these women function at a very high level.

Ruby was a woman in her late 20s who had a late diagnosis of high functioning autism. She lived on her own and attended a college where she was doing very well academically, and also contributed to the running of the college by being very active on many committees. Ruby had always had catatonia episodes since she was at school, but she did not realise what this was and coped. In adulthood, after experiencing exploitation and abuse in several relationships, she developed generalised anxiety, and also an increase in the severity and frequency of the catatonia episodes.

On some days, Ruby had severe difficulties in initiating movements, actions and speech and had episodes of getting 'frozen' such that she was unable to move, speak or complete motor actions. These episodes were very frightening for Ruby, and also could put her at considerable risk when she was on her own and unable to move. Some days, she was unable to get out of bed and thus was unable to eat, drink or attend college. On some days, she could get up after some time and managed to get to college but was often late.

## Nina

Nina's manifestations of catatonia, shutdown and breakdown were described in Chapter 3. A detailed assessment analysing retrospective information, Nina's underlying autism and vulnerability, and psycho-ecological factors indicated a possible cumulative effect of various potential contributory factors. These included:

- hormonal changes due to onset of puberty

- change-over to senior school which meant different demands

- additional changes of staff/teachers within the school

- changes in Nina's regular visits and relationship with her grandfather due to his illness

- increased time out of school, resulting in less structure, activity and stimulation

- increased risk of catatonia due to Nina being in the 'passive' subgroup of autism

- side effects of anti-psychotic medication (trial and error experimentation with powerful psychiatric medication had not helped but worsened Nina's catatonia).

This case example illustrates possible cumulative effects of various potential factors leading to gradual worsening of catatonia, especially without early diagnosis and appropriate psycho-ecological intervention to stop the downward spiral of cumulative factors.

# Chapter 6

# Intervention and Management Approaches

## AN OVERVIEW

As discussed throughout this book, catatonia in autistic people is a complex heterogeneous condition with many types of manifestations. There is a wide range of severity along several dimensions, and there is huge individual variation in terms of symptom manifestation, causes and needs. The treatment and management of these conditions needs to be based on multi-dimensional methods involving a range of approaches and professionals, depending on individual needs. Although historically the assessment and treatment of catatonia has followed a medical and psychiatric model, we have found that a non-medical psychological holistic approach is essential for understanding, assessing and treating autism-related catatonia. Thus, we have recommended a psychological and a psycho-ecological approach (Shah and Wing 2006). This approach can incorporate the medical/psychiatric treatment (short term) if necessary, and other multi-disciplinary therapies and strategies as relevant.

## Overview of different interventions

DeJong, Bunton and Hare (2014) carried out a systematic review of interventions used to treat catatonic symptoms in people with ASD. They identified the following approaches reported in the literature.

- Electroconvulsive therapy (ECT): the review identified 11 relevant papers with 12 cases reported.

- Pharmacological treatments using psychiatric medications: the study identified seven papers with a total of ten cases reported.

- Behavioural (psychological) interventions which included our Shah and Wing holistic psychological (Shah and Wing 2006) approach and one case study of a specific targeted behaviour intervention (Hare and Malone 2004).

- Sensory treatment which included packing therapy: this involves wrapping patients in damp sheets while inviting them to express their feelings and sensations to promote sensory integration. The study identified two papers involving three cases (Cohen *et al.* 2009; Consoli *et al.* 2010).

Their overall conclusions were that the quality of the literature with regard to interventions was poor with particular limitations in treatment description and outcome measurement. The majority of the papers were concerned with medical treatment using ECT and/or psychiatric medications.

## Medical interventions

There is a very limited literature of individual case reports and small case series describing effects of medical treatments of catatonia in autistic individuals. These report a range of psychiatric medications, doses and effects. Most of these reports concern severe, acute manifestation of catatonia in individuals with ASD. These have been documented and reviewed in the paper by DeJong *et al.* (2014). As pointed out by the authors, the outcomes should be interpreted cautiously for various reasons. There was a strong likelihood of reporting bias as many papers mentioned previously ineffective medical intervention. Generally, treatment was only partially effective with continuing fluctuations in symptoms and periodic episodes of catatonia. This is not surprising given the normal fluctuation of catatonia and the occurrence of episodic catatonia as discussed in Chapter 2.

As pointed out by Fink *et al.* (2006) and Zaw (2006), there is huge individual variation in response to medical treatments in autistic people who develop catatonia. Currently, benzodiazepines are the most frequently used medications for the treatment of severe catatonia (Dhossche *et al.* 2006b; Kakooza-Mwesige, Wachtel and Dhossche 2008; Mazzone *et al.* 2014).

Clinicians who use medication to treat catatonia symptoms in autism should do so with extreme caution and be mindful of the possibility of the side effects of the medication, which may trigger catatonia symptoms or make them worse. This has been discussed in detail in Chapter 5. Medication which is carefully tailored and monitored may be useful as an emergency treatment for acute severe catatonia or as a short-term treatment trial in selected cases. Before, during and after medical treatment, it is important to continue using the psycho-ecological approach and strategies for supporting the individuals and their families as described below. The importance of using medication for short-term intervention and using psychological and psycho-ecological strategies for long-term is recognised by medical practitioners involved in treating complex presentations of chronic catatonia in autistic people (Dhossche *et al.* 2006b; Mazzone *et al.* 2014).

## Electroconvulsive therapy (ECT)

In acute/severe cases, various psychiatrists have advocated the use of ECT (on its own or in combination with psychiatric medication), which has been described in case reports as having dramatic effects (Ghaziuddin *et al.* 2010; Wachtel, Hermida and Dhossche 2010). DeJong *et al.* (2014) in their review of case reports of ECT concluded that 'Despite assertions by several authors regarding the safety and efficacy of ECT in this population, the evidence underlying these assertions in weak' (p.2131). They also noted that 'the majority of the studies made no reference to the adverse effects of treatment. This is surprising, given the extensive literature that exists regarding reported side effects of ECT' (p.2130).

The use of ECT in psychiatry has been and remains hugely controversial. This is due to the known risk of side effects to memory and cognitive functioning and other risks associated. Zaw (2006) has provided an excellent summary of the concerns with regard to using ECT as a treatment for catatonia in young people with autism. As pointed out by Zaw (2006) and Fink *et al.* (2006), although ECT can be useful as a short-term treatment, it cannot be repeated often or be used as a long-term treatment.

In view of these difficulties, any clinician considering using ECT for a person with autism-related catatonia needs to be extremely cautious and mindful of the risks and adverse effects.

## Non-medical interventions

There is no systematic research-based study of non-medical intervention for catatonia in autistic individuals. DeJong *et al.* (2014) reviewed the few case reports available and concluded the following:

> Given the limited data available in this area, and the lack of high quality evidence, no clear conclusions can be drawn about the efficacy of behavioural and sensory interventions. Patients receiving packing therapy appeared to derive some short-term benefit, but the presence of various confounding interventions (medication, ward milieu etc.) precludes any clear conclusion as to the efficacy of this approach. Behavioural interventions seemed to provide some benefit, although symptoms resolved only partly in all cases. The number of cases described is also extremely small. The literature includes both specific, targeted interventions (Hare and Malone 2004) and more general supportive interventions (Shah and Wing 2006). These interventions include various components, and it remains unclear which are necessary to produce change. Further evaluation studies, including clear treatment protocols and objective measures of outcome, would be a valuable addition to the evidence base in the area. (p.2133)

## The psycho-ecological approach

We have developed a non-medical psychological holistic approach which has proved extremely useful for understanding, evaluating and treating catatonia and breakdown in autism (Shah and Wing 2006). DeJong *et al.* (2014) have referred to this as a general supportive approach in their review. It has also been referred to as the 'Shah and Wing approach' (Dossche *et al.* 2006). I have further extended this approach on the basis of extensive clinical experience and insight and now refer to it as a 'psycho-ecological approach'. This is based on my firm belief that the understanding, treatment and prevention of catatonia manifestations in the context of autism have to be moved from the historical medical/psychiatric model to the psychological arena.

It is worth considering briefly the differences in essence between a psychiatric/medical and a psychological approach in this context. Psychiatric approaches are based on finding the most appropriate diagnostic category to which the individual's symptoms can be assigned, and then finding a medical treatment which fits the category. This is essentially a categorical approach which is not concerned about the detailed profile or nature of the individual's symptoms/ difficulties or the causes and individual differences. Psychological approaches are dimensional rather than categorical, and are concerned with individual profiles to understand the person's presenting symptoms and difficulties. Detailed assessments, individual profiles and formulations about the underlying nature of the difficulties and possible causes, and individually tailored treatment and management are the cornerstone of the psychological approach. Psychologists draw on a large pool of psychological theories to guide their formulations and are concerned with the interactions between the underlying biological and psychological impairments and social and ecological factors. This is exactly what is needed for autistic individuals with catatonia and related shutdown and breakdown. Ecological factors refer to all aspects of the 'environment' which the individual has to cope with. These include physical and sensory environment, educational and occupational settings (e.g. mainstream/special), programme and lifestyle, social (e.g. relationships, peer pressure, demands and social media), culture and milieu.

The psycho-ecological approach described in this book has evolved through the author's clinical and research experience in autism, spanning four decades. It is based on a psychological understanding of an individual's autism and the significance of relevant ecological factors leading to distress, stress, anxiety and non-coping. Clinical experience and discussions with autistic individuals, their families, carers, teachers and local professionals involved in supporting them have been instrumental in developing this approach.

This is not a specific psychological treatment but a multi-dimensional, holistic approach based on a psychological framework of assessing the individual's specific presentation of difficulties and formulating an individual plan of intervention, management and support at various levels. The individual's difficulties have to be assessed and understood in the context of their underlying autism and needs, and their individual manifestation of the catatonia. This approach is about identifying relevant individual management and support strategies which vary for individuals and their families/carers/local professionals. The underlying causes for each individual's breakdown in the form of catatonia are complex and differ for individuals, and these need to be identified by understanding the individual's profile of autism and needs. The psycho-ecological approach is described in detail in the next chapter.

# Chapter 7

# The Psycho-Ecological Approach

This chapter discusses in detail the components of the psycho-ecological approach and the Shah 4 Stage Implementation Model.

## Main components of the psycho-ecological approach

I. Psychological and ecological assessment and formulation

II. Identifying individual stress, anxiety and non-coping

III. Increasing awareness and avoiding misdiagnosis

IV. Psycho-education and training

V. Reviewing and withdrawing 'culprit' psychiatric medication

VI. Early identification

VII. Increasing structure, routine and consistency

VIII. Implementing immediate strategies of support

IX. Activity and stimulation therapy

X. Reducing decision making

XI. Management of specific problems

XII. Psychological interventions and support for high functioning autistic individuals

# I. Psychological and ecological assessment and formulation

The most important component of the psycho-ecological approach is to carry out a detailed psychological and ecological assessment based on dimensional methods. This is discussed below.

## 1. Profile of catatonia, shutdown and breakdown

Use the Autism Catatonia Evaluation (ACE-S) in Appendix 1 supplemented by additional information to build up an individual's profile on the following:

- manifestation of the different aspects of catatonia, shutdown and breakdown

- fluctuations and variations

- secondary difficulties

- effects on functioning and quality of life

- deterioration of functioning

- strategies which are effective

- amount of help/support which the person needs and can tolerate

- activities and interests – past and present.

## 2. Profile of individual's autism and vulnerability

This is a comprehensive detailed assessment based on information collated from various sources and methods. This includes observations and psychometric assessment, interviews with parents/carers/teachers using semi-structured methods, perusal of past and present relevant reports and viewing of video clips (if applicable). The assessment would have to be adapted to each individual and their situation. The following list is a guide for the type of information which is useful in compiling a psychological profile of the individual in the context of catatonia, shutdown and breakdown.

- relevant developmental history with emphasis on early regression, sensitivity and overlapping autism/catatonia features, change over time

- pattern of social interaction/impairment with emphasis on evidence of passivity, sociability, relationships and tolerance of social demands

- communication ability and profile with emphasis on special methods/devices to enhance the individual's communication

- pattern of stereotypic and repetitive behaviours

- sensory likes and dislikes

- mood fluctuations, emotions and arousal levels

- perceptual/cognitive style

- likes, dislikes and motivating factors

- past and present behaviour patterns

- past ways of expressing frustration, anger, and negative emotions

- highest level of independence reached on self-care skills and community functioning

- strengths, general and special interests, and activities enjoyed.

Psychometric assessment is useful for quantitative information regarding cognitive functioning and profile, and qualitative observations such as attention, concentration, focus and engagement. It is important to use non-verbal tests if the person is not able to speak generally or due to catatonia.

### 3. Ecological and milieu factors
Ecological factors refer to all aspects of the 'environment' and the 'milieu' which the individual has to cope with. These include physical and sensory environment, educational and occupational settings (e.g. mainstream/special), programme and lifestyle, social factors such as relationships, peer group, demands and effects of social media.

An assessment of the person's environment (social and physical), programme and daily occupation is important in order to match the suitability and demands to the person's pattern of autism and their needs. Social networks, peer group and social media factors also need to be considered with regard to the demands made on the individual.

As discussed in Chapter 5, the causes of stress, distress and non-coping leading to catatonia, shutdown and breakdown are often external aspects to do with the ecological factors. This can only be worked out by understanding the person's autism and needs and looking at the mismatch between their needs and the environment and milieu factors.

## ASSESSMENT OF ECOLOGICAL AND MILIEU FACTORS

This assessment is individually tailored and structured. The following considerations are not comprehensive but may be helpful as suggestions for the kind of environmental and milieu factors which may be important to consider and be vigilant about:

- Does the person have a service, or are they at home without daily structured occupation? Many autistic people have developed a catatonia-related breakdown after leaving school when they stayed at home without any structured occupation, routine and organised external activities.

- Is the service autism specific? Does it have autism-friendly systems and an autism-friendly environment? It is important not to make assumptions that the programme and service is suitable for the autistic individual just because it is supposed to be autism specific.

- Is the level of structure, routine, consistency and predictability suitable for the individual's needs?

- Is the programme suitable for their level of autism and ability (bearing in mind that autistic individuals can have an uneven profile of cognitive ability)? Is the level of stimulation and demand too much or too little?

- Are there factors which are overwhelming, frightening or stress and anxiety provoking (for example, noise, chaos, too much going on, size of group, type of peer group)?

- Consider the possibility of negative social experiences such as feeling out of depth, not coping, bullying, violence and exploitation. Family and friends of autistic people should be vigilant as the autistic individual is unlikely to be able to communicate these experiences or take themselves out of the situation until it is too late. (This is where the earlier section on early identification and picking up early signs of difficulties and non-coping is important to understand and apply.)

- Is the client:staffing ratio appropriate for the person's needs? Many people who have developed a catatonia-related breakdown need one-to-one support initially, and then a small group approach with a high staff ratio.

- If the individual is at school, college or university, it is important to assess particular demands which could be overwhelming them.

- Is the individual trying to cope in settings beyond their capacity, for example, being in mainstream settings without support and feeling overwhelmed? Many autistic people have had a breakdown in these circumstances, for example attending courses at mainstream college after leaving school, being at university without special needs support or trying to cope in employment without special adjustments or support.

- Consider the decreased threshold for tolerance of stress at certain times, and increase support to reduce the impact of ecological factors, for example, puberty, transitions, changes in family composition, bereavement and house move.

## 4. Interpretation and formulation

The most important aspect of the psychological assessment is the interpretation and analysis of the information to make a detailed individual formulation. This can confirm the diagnosis, and describe the individual manifestations and patterns of difficulties relating to catatonia, shutdown and breakdown. The interaction between the person's needs due to autism and the ecological factors will have to be analysed to suggest possible causes, and to make an individual plan of management using the principles and strategies of the psycho-ecological approach described above. Individual-informed formulation and detailed recommendations for a holistic, multi-dimensional plan of intervention, management and support are the most crucial aspects. This  is a qualitative and creative process which requires clinical expertise and experience in autism, and a certain amount of clinical intuition.

## II. Identifying individual stress, anxiety and non-coping

An important aspect of the psycho-ecological approach in treating autism-related catatonia and maintaining the progress and preventing relapse is to identify possible ongoing stressors which are affecting the person.

This aspect has been covered in detail in Chapter 5, and protocols and guidance for assessment are described in detail in the section above on psychological and ecological assessment and formulation.

The case examples in Chapter 8 on the application of the psycho-ecological approach illustrate how this component works in practice.

## III. Increasing awareness and avoiding misdiagnosis

One of the main difficulties with catatonia-related breakdown in autistic people is that it often gets missed, misdiagnosed or inappropriately conceptualised.

One of the essential components of this approach has been to raise awareness of catatonia-related breakdown in autistic people. This is crucial in order to enable carers and professionals to conceptualise it as catatonia-related difficulties as early as possible, and for professionals to avoid misdiagnosing it. This will help to prevent management errors which can exacerbate the difficulties and lead to more severe manifestations.

Unfortunately, very often well-meaning carers and professionals start doing the exact opposite of what the person needs when they have an onset of catatonia-related breakdown:

- With regard to medication, instead of withdrawing possible 'culprit' medication, often additional medication is prescribed to 'help' the person either as a result of misdiagnosis or as a trial and error approach.

- The person is given less support rather than more as staff want them to remain independent and feel if they leave the person, they will get back to how they could function previously.

For example, even if the person is having difficulty with eating and is taking hours to finish a meal, they are not given help.

- Pressure is put on the person either by not believing them, not validating their difficulties or accusing them of being lazy, manipulative or wilful.

- The person starts getting excluded from activities which they used to enjoy, and which it is crucial to keep going.

- Often, the decision is taken to stop the person from attending activities, day centre and so on rather than putting in support and strategies to enable them to continue. This results in loss of structure and routine and inactivity, all of which are likely to exacerbate the breakdown in someone with autism. Sometimes, however, it may be necessary to withdraw the person from the activities and the education/occupation/ residential environment to enable them to recover in a stress-free environment (e.g. home), and gradually build up their activity and transition to a more suitable 'environment'.

## IV. Psycho-education and training

Psycho-education and training is useful at various levels:

- In promoting general awareness and understanding of this complex condition.

- In enabling carers, professionals and service providers to understand the nature and manifestations of the condition in a particular individual. A common shared conceptualisation is most important.

- In enabling carers and local professionals to find proactive strategies and solutions. Psychological techniques of cognitive restructuring are important for carers as this can lead to positive and different expectations which can significantly affect their management of the individual.

- In enabling parents/carers to implement appropriate management strategies from the outset.

- To enable high functioning individuals to recognise the symptoms, and develop their own strategies for preventing episodes, coping and reducing the impact of the catatonia.

## V. Reviewing and withdrawing 'culprit' psychiatric medication

This is one of the most important management strategies for someone who shows any signs of developing autism-related catatonia. As discussed above, one of the causes can be the side effects of some psychiatric medications. If the person has been prescribed any medication with possible motor and extra-pyramidal side effects, the professionals concerned should immediately consider gradual withdrawal of the medication. This may alleviate the symptoms and reverse catatonia-related breakdown if it is detected at an early stage, and also if the person has not been on the medication for long, or if the person has not been on a complex 'cocktail' of psychiatric medications.

Unfortunately, very often the medication withdrawal in itself will not be enough, and this will have to be done in conjunction with other management strategies described below. Some individuals may show complex withdrawal symptoms which will need careful interpretation and management and extra support.

## VI. Early identification

As described above, the onset of catatonia-related breakdown in autistic people is gradual, and usually starts off mildly. If it is picked up at an early stage it can be reversed with appropriate intervention and management. Usually, the following are early signs which should alert carers and professionals that something is not working for the individual and investigate possible problems. At the same time they should provide support as detailed below.

Early signs to watch out for:

- slowness – this can apply to movements or actions or speech

- having brief 'freezing' or 'shutdown' episodes

- decline in engagement and interest

- deterioration in any aspect of functioning or skills

- an increase in passivity

- becoming more withdrawn and less communicative.

## VII. Increasing structure, routine and consistency

It is necessary to check and ensure that basic principles of good autism management are being applied at the level necessary for the individual to feel secure, stable and calm. These include structure at various levels, a good routine, predictability, consistency and individual communication systems if necessary. It is often necessary to tighten up the structure even more, keep to a more regular routine and increase predictability to enable the autistic individual with catatonia and related breakdown to recover. Often, providing one-to-one support from a small group of consistent people can provide security, stability, predictability and consistency and enable the individual to start recovering while other changes are being planned and implemented.

Unfortunately, educational or residential and day-care services which are supposed to be specialist for autistic individuals do not always implement these autism-friendly principles at the level necessary.

## VIII. Implementing immediate strategies of support
### 1. Support, assistance and help

It is extremely important that the person should be given support, assistance and as much help as they need to complete activities and to keep to their routine as much as possible. Although this seems obvious, parents and staff are often unsure as to how much help to give a person and how much to leave them to their own devices. I have come across very well-meaning parents, carers or teachers who have left the individual to complete activities like eating, washing and dressing even if it is taking hours to complete. They, understandably, find it difficult to provide help and assistance to an individual who has been independent previously. I cannot emphasise enough how important it is to provide the help and support and to keep the person moving through their routine of activities through the day.

## 2. Prompting, cognitive refocusing (distraction) and other strategies

One of the intriguing aspects about catatonia is the positive effect of an external stimulus in enabling movement and action. When the person is 'stuck' and unable to move or to complete an action, the problem is due to an internal system of initiating action. Yet, often, with an external stimulus in the form of a verbal or a physical prompt, the person is often able to get 'unstuck' and complete actions and movements and may not require another prompt for a long time unless they get stuck again. In more severe cases, the person may need constant prompts for each bit of movement and action, especially on 'bad' days.

The general principle is to provide as much prompting, help or physical assistance as a person needs to carry out movements and actions smoothly.

Verbal prompts may be minimal, for instance saying the person's name, or they may involve full instructions. Verbal instructions can be counterproductive as often the person with autism finds it intrusive and too much information to process. Verbal instructions to move or to carry out a particular action also draw too much attention to the movement required, and this may sometimes exacerbate the 'freezing'.

Physical prompting or helping, done casually without drawing attention to the 'freezing', often works much better. If a person 'freezes' while walking often a light tap on the shoulder or linking arms with the person can be effective. If the freezing occurs during an activity, a light touch at the elbow may be enough.

At times, a picture or photo card depicting an activity on the person's timetable can work better than a physical or a verbal prompt. For autistic people who do not use a visual communication system, an object of reference can be used to prompt them to the next activity.

Other strategies to enable the person to overcome 'freezing' and become 'unstuck' may have to be used. For someone who becomes more and more anxious and thus more stuck with direct prompting, it may be better to try a cognitive refocusing strategy instead of prompting. For example, for someone who is verbal, it may be effective to keep talking to them about general things, or offer them a beanbag to catch, or something to hold and manipulate. For some people music, sensory objects, an unusual sound or particular pictures or photos have been helpful. Different things and several strategies may have to be tried to find one which works in different situations for the individual.

One mother of a young autistic man who had fluctuating catatonic episodes reported:

> When he was first experiencing severe catatonia, he was switching in and out of it frequently and the strangest distractions would bring him out of it. One time it was a small crab in his hand as we walked on a beach – he had been following me like a robot, withdrawn, head down with a stiff gait, but the minute he set eyes on the crab and felt it on his hand, something clicked and within seconds, he was back to his usual self, relaxed and fluid in his movements, chatting and happy.

This young man had an affinity with animals and so the crab worked wonders for him as a cognitive refocusing strategy. It is as if for him, the deep connection which he feels with animals enabled him to reboot and refresh his cognitive/emotional focus.

Care should be taken, however, not to increase the person's anxiety when trying cognitive refocusing/distraction strategies. An approach which is often tried by staff is to provide 'intensive interaction' to engage the person who is showing aloofness or 'switching off' due to the catatonia-related breakdown. This can be extremely anxiety provoking and is usually counterproductive for the management of catatonia-related breakdown.

Many high functioning autistic individuals who live alone and have periodic episodes of 'freezing' do not always have someone around who can provide the prompting which they need. We have tried to investigate whether some form of automated message would be effective. Unfortunately, automated messages, timers and buzzers do not have the same effect and in fact seem to increase anxiety and the 'freezing'. One high functioning autistic individual has used the text to voice app on her phone. During a freezing episode, if she is able to use her fingers, she slowly types in a message to give herself a prompt. The converted voice message on her phone has enabled her to get moving again. The same individual also worked out an elaborate eye blink code with her boyfriend to enable her to communicate to him which prompt was useful when she was unable to talk during a catatonic episode. Interestingly, this couple worked out this system of prompts before they even realised that these were episodes of catatonia.

### 3. One-to-one support

Providing one-to-one support to the individual is effective and beneficial at various levels. It provides security and reassurance to the person that they will not be left in a 'paralytic' state (which must be very frightening and stressful in itself). The individual can be provided with the optimal prompting and external strategies to enable them to complete movements and to keep active. The one-to-one support enables individuals with autism-related catatonia to engage in constructive activity and to maintain or develop a conducive daily routine with structure and stimulation.

The consistency and quality of one-to-one support is important for it to be beneficial. Autistic individuals in general and especially those with catatonia are sensitive to the qualitative aspects of the interaction and approach used by the one-to-one support; this is a very important consideration when applying the psycho-ecological approach. In general, one-to-one support should be provided by as few people as is practically possible.

## IX. Activity and stimulation therapy

One of the most basic and important therapeutic strategies is to keep the individual active, engaged and stimulated in activities they enjoy. This may need intensive support, organisation and imagination initially to find suitable activities and settings. The individual's engagement and participation may have to be built up gradually. The importance of activity, stimulation and engagement therapy cannot be overemphasised and is usually more beneficial and therapeutic for overcoming catatonia and related breakdown than other psychological therapies.

One parent explained this with regard to her son with severe fluctuating catatonia:

> My son has had various therapies such as cognitive behaviour therapy, solution focused therapy and exposure techniques and counselling. None of these have had any benefits and have often caused more harm than good. By far the most powerful 'therapy' for him has always been being involved in enjoyable activities, for example, lunch out, cream teas, cinema, walks in the woods, bowling, voluntary work with animals, etc.

It is all too common and easy for the individual's activities to reduce so that gradually their activity level and quality of life drop significantly. Many people with catatonia-related breakdown start spending gradually longer times in bed, in their bedroom, in the bathroom or toilet, or on only self-directed repetitive activities on which they get 'stuck'. Parents and carers often report that the individual concerned is 'refusing' to come out to participate in activities or outings which they used to enjoy.

As with everything else with this condition, it is easier to intervene and get the person engaged in a programme of activities if the problem is recognised at an early stage. The following strategies have been tried and have worked for different individuals:

- Start by using the activities which the person has enjoyed the most, or any activity on which they seem most motivated currently. Use any activity which sparks off even the slightest interest. Link an activity that you want the person to engage in to their favourite activity. For example, after Lee developed catatonia-related breakdown, the only activity which motivated him and he enjoyed was a trip to his favourite burger place (referred to here as Jack's). This had been one of his favourite activities previously. After he slowed down and became less active, staff began to bring him his favourite Jack's meal as a take-away rather than taking him there. They were advised to change this and take Lee to Jack's even if it meant using the wheelchair on days when he was having significant difficulty with walking. Gradually, other activities were added in before and after the Jack's trip, and Lee became more active and started enjoying a full daily programme of activities again.

- Try activities which are more physical, outdoors and active rather than table-top activities. Many autistic individuals find it therapeutic to spend time outdoors and connecting with nature and animals. Often, when someone develops catatonia-related breakdown, they become more housebound due to difficulties in walking and so on. This results in them being unable to pursue the very activities which were meaningful and pleasurable for them. For example, after Ria developed catatonia-related breakdown, she was unable to attend day services and enjoy the interaction with others and her favourite craft activities. She became housebound as she became increasingly fearful of going outdoors. Ria was also unable to enjoy nature and community activities which had previously brought her a lot of joy. Staff were advised to use any strategies possible to enable Ria to pursue nature and community activities. The main problem was Ria's mobility due to muscle wasting and fear. Once this was made a priority, staff found various ways to transport Ria to places where she could engage in activities which gave her joy. This had a huge beneficial effect generally on Ria's catatonia symptoms which decreased substantially, and improved her quality of life.

- Avoid activities and environments which are known to trigger more catatonia-related episodes.

- It is often helpful to start the person's day with their favourite physical activity. This can get them going and reduce the overall impact of the catatonia for the rest of the day. For example, Steve used to love swimming which he used to do three times a week in a community pool. After he developed catatonia-related breakdown it was considered too risky to take him swimming in case he got stuck in the showers or in the swimming pool. After a risk assessment and plan, staff were advised to reinstate Steve's swimming in a supervised hydro-therapy pool which had a hoist to aid people with physical disabilities. As Steve had become totally inactive and had severe catatonia-related difficulties, staff were advised to carry out the swimming session as a first activity every morning. This was highly successful. Steve never showed any catatonia 'freezing' in the pool, and this was instrumental in getting him to become more active and overcome the catatonia-related breakdown. Other changes were also made to his medication and living environment and programme which all helped to maintain his recovery and avoided a repeat of the breakdown.

- Activities with definite targets can sometimes be very effective in getting the person concerned to aim for, and can act as an external prompt which enables them to make fluid movements.

Examples of such activities include ten-pin bowling, skittles, catching ball/beanbag, darts, inset jigsaw puzzles and colouring defined pictures.

- Passive activities such as watching television, a DVD, listening to music or sitting in a car for long journeys can be detrimental as often the person with catatonia-related breakdown tends to switch off, or go into repetitive movements. It is generally more beneficial to have activities which involve some action on the part of the individual interspersed with relaxing activities which are more passive, for example music and car rides.

- Cognitive stimulation is vital. It is important to remember that a person who develops catatonia-related breakdown comes across as having slowed down and regressed in their skills. Although regression does occur in some people, most people with catatonia-related breakdown are cognitively alert and would be functioning at the same level intellectually as they did before the onset of the catatonia-related breakdown. Thus, it is important that carers and professionals do not underestimate their intellectual functioning and offer stimulating activities of the type they have enjoyed previously.

## X. Reducing decision making

The ability to make decisions and choose between options seems to get worse in many autistic individuals when they develop catatonia. It is helpful and actually beneficial to the individual if other people make the decisions on their behalf. The dilemma of making a choice or a decision seems to cause stress and anxiety and can increase shutdown and freezing. Reducing or removing choice goes against the principles of humanistic, positive support and care providing so understandably, carers and professionals feel unsure and uncomfortable applying this recommendation. However, this becomes easier when they understand the reasons and are reassured that it will help the individual and that they can gradually increase choices when they make progress. A gradual approach of limited options can be introduced and progressed according to the individual's ability to cope with decision making.

# XI. Management of specific problems

The following are some pointers for dealing with some specific problems.

## 1. Eating problems

Many individuals with catatonia develop severe difficulties with eating. The complex motor coordination required for eating with a knife and fork or with a spoon seems to trigger particular severe difficulties in initiating and completing movements and ritualistic and repetitive behaviour. There are also difficulties with the movements of lips, jaws and tongue required to take the food off the fork or spoon and to chew and swallow it.

The eating difficulties are often misinterpreted as 'playing up', being deliberately slow or having a poor appetite. Parents and carers may be advised by professionals involved not to be concerned, to leave the individual to eat if they want to and when they want to. The result is often severe loss of weight and an exacerbation of the other aspects of catatonia.

The problems can be reduced by using verbal and physical prompts and by making the process of feeding as easy for the individual as possible. Depending on the extent of the difficulties, any of the following methods may have to be used:

- A spoon can be used instead of a knife and fork.

- The type and consistency of food can be adjusted so that it is easily scooped onto a spoon.

- Verbal prompts can be given for each action required or for each mouthful.

- Physical prompts can be used ranging from touching the elbow lightly to giving hand-on-hand support and guiding the individual's movements in the direction required.

- If prompts are not sufficient, the individual may have to be fed.

- If the individual is having difficulty opening the mouth, a light touch on the cheek or touching the lips with the loaded spoon may be effective.

- The individual may find it more difficult and stressful to eat in a group situation or a noisy environment. Relevant adjustments need to be made to address this.

## 2. Speech and communication problems

The planning and execution of the movements required for speech are as difficult for a person with catatonia as any other motor activity. It is important not to put pressure on the individual to answer questions or to talk. Instead, others should talk to the individual focusing on the current activity. It is more important to relate to the individual through physical activities than through verbal discussions.

Having to verbalise choices is particularly difficult for people with ASD and this is exacerbated by the motor problems of catatonia. Carers may need to make the decisions and choices for the individual on the basis of their knowledge of the person, their interests and their likes and dislikes. Using gentle suggestion and encouragement, without asking directly what the individual wants to do or whether or not they want to do something, is the most helpful approach.

## 3. Difficulty with walking

The individual will be able to walk without stopping if they are holding on to or linking with the carer's arm. If the individual stops suddenly, a light physical prompt on the back or a verbal prompt will help them to start again. Sometimes, walking as part of a group enables the individual to walk at a steady pace without stopping.

## 4. Incontinence

Individuals with catatonia often show signs of incontinence. This is usually related to the difficulty of getting up from a chair or bed and reaching the toilet in time, or the inability to ask to go to the toilet. Such incontinence is puzzling and distressing for an individual who previously was fully independent in this respect. This needs to be understood and managed in a discreet and sensitive way.

Simple methods, such as regular, frequent physical and/or verbal prompts to go to the toilet and giving enough time to use the toilet are useful. The individual may need assistance with clothes and then be given a verbal prompt to use the toilet. Depending on the severity of catatonia, the individual may need physical assistance with personal hygiene.

Individuals with severe catatonia who have difficulty using the toilet independently will benefit from a regular toilet use programme. The use of the toilet should be linked to the daily routine by slotting it in at appropriate times, such as immediately on waking up, at the beginning and end of each period of activity, before or after each mealtime and before going to bed. This will work only if there is a consistent daily routine that is pre-planned and adhered to as strictly as possible.

As the individual makes progress, the amount of prompting and physical assistance should be adjusted accordingly.

## 5. Standing still or adopting fixed postures

Fixed postures of any kind will be extremely tiring for the muscles, but the individual will not be able to express this or do anything about it.

The individual who appears to be standing still and staring into space is probably unable to initiate movement needed for a particular activity. A verbal prompt or a light touch may enable them to move. They should then be involved immediately in a different activity. At times, the individual may raise one or both arms and be unable to bring them down for long periods. They need to be helped by their carer bringing the arms down physically.

## 6. Catatonic excitement

Episodes of uncontrollable, frenzied and inappropriate behaviour may occur. These are often thought by carers to be outbursts of 'challenging' behaviour. This misconception leads to an endless and irrelevant search for 'triggers' and 'functions' and the application of behavioural methods to stop the inappropriate behaviours. In the clinical experience of the author, this has not proved to be a useful approach for the management of catatonic excitement. Even more unhelpful is telling the person to stop behaving in that way, to stop being silly or asking them why they are doing this.

If these episodes are short lived and do not affect the safety of the individual or of others or of the environment, the best strategy may be not to intervene, though supervising to ensure safety, and then to give support when the incident is finished.

If the episodes are more severe and longer lasting, intervention at different levels may help the individual to calm down more quickly. Verbal suggestions to do something different, mild physical restraint or simply physically leading the person into a different environment and making them sit down may work. Different strategies are needed to suit different individuals. When the episode is over, the individual should be reassured and encouraged to carry on with the normal routine.

These episodes will reduce in frequency and severity as the effects of catatonia decrease and the individual makes progress.

## XII. Psychological interventions and support for high functioning autistic individuals

As part of an overall psycho-ecological approach, the following psychological intervention strategies and support can be beneficial. These can be used with the individual themselves, or together with family members or trusted friend/carer. Some individuals will not be able to use the following strategies themselves, and will need support at different levels from others in their lives.

- Psychological and ecological assessment (as described in section I above) and formulation about possible factors causing stress, distress, anxiety and non-coping can be used. Also useful is psycho-education and discussion to enable the person to understand what the autism means for them, their vulnerability to stress and non-coping, and to empower them to make changes in their life and develop coping strategies.

- It can be helpful to use instruction in increasing self-awareness and self-management of anxiety and stress and to develop coping strategies for different situations. Developing a 'resource and strategies' box to draw from and use during difficult situations can be beneficial.

- Individuals can benefit from training in active relaxation (through activities, hobbies and interests) and cognitive refocusing techniques, for example by focusing on neutral activities and building up an 'activities/ideas box' to use to 'reboot' and 'refresh' self and refocus.

- Enabling the individual to recognise early signs of shutdown in themselves and strategies for getting out of stressful environments and situations or allowing a brief period of 'shutdown' to recover can be helpful.

- General psychological interventions such as cognitive behaviour therapy (adapted for autism) or dialectical behaviour therapy may be useful for some individuals. However, most autistic individuals who develop catatonia, shutdown and breakdown are likely to find such therapies too intense and stressful in terms of social interaction and communication demands.

- Some individuals may benefit from using computerised anxiety management apps which are available for the self-management of anxiety for individuals with anxiety.

- Techniques from holistic approaches and therapies such as yoga, meditation, reflexology, mindfulness or prayanama (breathing exercises based on ancient Indian methods) may be useful for some individuals to learn and add to their resource box.

## The Shah 4 Stage Implementation Model

This is based on a model developed by the author in clinical practice for advising on the management and services for autistic individuals with severe 'challenging behaviour'. It has been adapted to guide implementation stages of the psycho-ecological approach described in this book.

---

**The Model**

Stage 1 – Response

Stage 2 – Short-term strategies

Stage 3 – Long-term strategies and management plan

Stage 4 – Monitoring and maintenance

---

## Stage 1 – Response

This stage constitutes the response when catatonia, shutdown and/or breakdown are detected or even suspected in any individual with autism. I would recommend to parents, carers and teachers to implement

Stage 1 even while they are awaiting diagnosis and professional support. Use ACE-S as guidance:

- conceptualise as possible catatonia-related breakdown
- support and help the individual
- provide prompts to encourage smooth movements
- maintain activities and programme
- maintain routine and structure
- reduce 'slowness' by giving extra help
- give as much one-to-one support as possible
- adopt a positive, supportive client-centred approach.

## Stage 2 – Short-term strategies

This stage incorporates involving professionals, assessing the manifestation of the catatonia-related breakdown, observations and consultation and putting in short-term strategies. The main elements are:

- involving professionals
- confirming diagnosis and severity
- assessing manifestation and details of catatonia-related breakdown
- assessing secondary effects and managing these
- assessing the effects/impact of catatonia-related breakdown
- reviewing medication and finding 'culprit' medications and taking action to withdraw if necessary
- reducing/eliminating any obvious stress- or anxiety-causing factors
- maintaining activity, structure and routine
- providing prompts, support and help as in Stage 1
- give as much one-to-one support as possible.

## Stage 3 – Long-term strategies and management plan

This stage requires the involvement of professionals to make an informed and detailed assessment of the individual's autism and stress factors and to make a comprehensive plan of management with changes as required.

The main components of this stage are as follows:

- detailed psychological assessment of the person's profile of autism

- detailed ecological assessment of environment and milieu factors

- formulation

- other assessments as necessary

- comprehensive plan of intervention, care and support

- written plan and guidelines

- full implementation of the psycho-ecological approach

- continue with Stage 1 elements and additional support

- tailor-made psycho-education and training

- change or make a care plan in light of the diagnosis of catatonia and its effects on the individual and the family

- agreed written plan for crisis intervention if necessary

- appoint a case manager who can coordinate the implementation.

## Stage 4 – Monitoring and maintenance

This is an extremely important stage for reviewing and maintaining progress, preventing relapse, updating new staff/carers/teachers and keeping up the programme and changes made. I have noted in various services how initial implementations of recommendations can all falter over time either through complacency, loss of urgency, staff changes, and so on. The person concerned invariably suffers and the catatonia-related breakdown can re-emerge or the person stops making progress or regresses.

The important elements of this stage are the following:

- regular checks and reviews of medication and avoiding 'culprits' creeping in

- regular meetings between carers and professionals

- reviewing and updating written guidelines

- reviewing and planning for changing needs as the person improves

- monitoring progress on care plan and resolving stumbling blocks such as funding

- keeping a check on signs of deterioration

- having an alert plan for early identification of anxiety/stress

- making changes to the management plan

- planning for crisis intervention

- checking on complacency creeping in.

# Chapter 8

# Application of the Psycho-Ecological Approach

The psycho-ecological approach described in detail in the last chapter can be applied at various different levels to help individuals and families to prevent and overcome the difficulties of catatonia, to address the secondary consequences and effects of the breakdown, and to improve the quality of life for individuals and their families. It can be applied minimally to improve understanding and conceptualisation of the individual's difficulties as catatonia, shutdown and breakdown. This can be achieved through increased awareness and knowledge through psycho-education and training. This in itself can sometimes be enough to gain clarity on formulation and achieve changes in care and management which can have positive outcomes. It can be applied to implement the immediate strategies while a diagnosis and further assessment and intervention advice is being sought. The principles of the psycho-ecological approach can be used to guide assessment, diagnosis and formulation to make a plan of intervention, support and management. Different components of the psycho-ecological approach may be useful at different times for an individual.

In my clinical experience, the correct diagnosis, formulation and a plan of management based on the principles of the psycho-ecological approach described in this book have always been helpful and have had overall positive effects. There is a lot of variation in terms of specific outcomes with regard to recovery from the catatonia manifestations and the secondary effects and breakdown. In many individuals, if there is timely diagnosis and formulation together with family and professional support to implement strategies and a management plan, total recovery is possible and the individual can remain free of catatonia episodes. In some people, the catatonia aspects get better quickly but it takes a lot longer to recover from the secondary effects and the consequences of breakdown. Some individuals overcome the catatonia difficulties and enjoy a good quality of life, but do not get back to their original level of functioning and achievement. In some individuals, the catatonia and breakdown are due to a complex mix of causes including side effects and/or withdrawal effects of psychiatric drugs and there are huge intervention and management challenges. For some, the prognosis is dependent on the provision of adequate services and effective professional backing and support. Sometimes, in residential settings, the success of the implementation of the psycho-ecological strategies depends on the acumen of the staff team and managers, and the ethos of the organisation.

The case studies below illustrate some applications of the psycho-ecological approach and the varied types of intervention and management strategies which are necessary and effective in achieving change for different individuals.

## Ricky
### Background
The background and details of the catatonia-related breakdown and possible causes for Ricky are given in Chapter 5.

### Application of the psycho-ecological approach
This was multi-dimensional and included the following:

- diagnosis of ASD and catatonia-related breakdown
- detailed assessment including cognitive assessment which indicated uneven profile and mild learning difficulty
- psycho-education for family and local professionals regarding how the autism and catatonia were affecting Ricky
- implementation of the immediate strategies of prompting, support and cognitive refocusing
- discussions with local professionals to revise formulation and care plan

- review of psychiatric medication and withdrawal

- one-to-one support worker for three sessions a week, started at home and then gradually at a day centre so that Ricky could attend small group activities (the one-to-one support was gradually withdrawn as Ricky improved)

- family intervention – advice on positively re-engaging Ricky in family activities and outings he had enjoyed previously using a non-confrontational, gentle approach

- a daily structured plan and routine enabling Ricky to revert to a more normal day and night time routine

- implementation of a long-term plan.

## Outcome

Ricky recovered from the catatonia and other aspects of his breakdown quickly once the above was implemented. He bounced back to his original self and became even happier and more motivated than before. Ricky had actually struggled in mainstream settings and had suffered a lot of bullying and trauma as a result. Due to his autism and passivity and risk of catatonia-related breakdown, he needed special rather than mainstream settings to achieve his potential and enjoy a good quality of life. Ricky went from strength to strength and went to live in a residential community for people with learning difficulties. The owner and manager of this service took a special interest in Ricky and enabled him to attend special courses at a local college and eventually get a part-time job. Ricky still keeps in touch with us and it is a joy to see him initiating contact, and hear about his achievements and all the social functions he attends and enjoys.

## Alice
### Background

Alice has a diagnosis of autism and learning disability. She was discussed briefly in Chapter 5 with regard to possible causes for her breakdown. Alice has the most delightful, responsive and cheerful personality. In spite of her autism, she is very people focused and very responsive when others initiate interaction. She makes strong attachments and responds well to encouragement, praise and distraction. The other side to this is that she is also very sensitive to how people are around her. People around her can provide comfort, security and feeling of wellbeing, or they can instil fear and stress in her.

## Details of Alice's catatonia and breakdown

Alice had movement difficulties associated with catatonia since the age of 15 years, but these had been manageable and had not impacted on her quality of life and activity level. At the age of 38 years Alice developed more severe catatonia and breakdown which had a major impact on her quality of life, activities and skills. These included the following:

- severe and long-lasting freezing episodes, with Alice sometimes becoming stuck and unable to move from a position for several hours

- becoming rigid and stiff and unable to move, especially when coming across changes in floor colour, pattern or texture; stopping abruptly mid-movement

- being unable to speak at times

- eating difficulties and becoming incontinent.

## Consequences and effects on quality of life

Alice became housebound and was no longer able to attend group day activities. She missed out on social interaction with others which she enjoyed and also stopped doing her favourite craft activities at which she was skilled. Alice was unable to enjoy nature and community activities which used to give her a lot of joy. She declined in her independence and developed fears and insecurities.

# Application of the psycho-ecological approach
## Comprehensive dimensional assessment based on the following

- individual psychological assessment of Alice based on observations and psychometric assessment

- observations of Alice in different situations including structured one-to-one situations, outings with staff and with parents, unstructured time in her home and activities with staff

- interviews with parents and staff members using relevant sections of the DISCO and ACE-S

- perusal of relevant reports and documents.

### Diagnosis and formulation

The diagnosis of autism-related catatonia and breakdown was confirmed. The formulation was based on an assessment and understanding of Alice's autism, personality, sensitivity and vulnerability, and the environment and situations she had to cope with. Alice had experienced autistic stress, distress, fear and trauma due to being in a crowded, noisy and unsafe living environment and witnessing and experiencing aggression from a fellow resident. Due to her passivity and communication difficulties, she had been unable to express these feelings and had a breakdown with shutdown and catatonia.

### Psycho-education and training

This involved training sessions with parents, staff and local professionals to discuss the results and formulation and to provide psycho-education on autism catatonia and how Alice was affected by this and the implications. This was supplemented by staff attending further training on autism catatonia and the psycho-ecological approach.

### Strategies for reducing freezing episodes and movement difficulties

This included the use of verbal prompts, physical prompts, cognitive refocusing by distraction, and cue cards. Advice was given about managing specific difficulties such as becoming stuck at transitions and walking on different surfaces, such as a manhole cover. An important strategy was not to focus on the difficulty, but to focus Alice's attention on getting to a goal, and looking ahead instead of down. The staff were asked not to focus or talk to Alice about why she was stuck but to encourage her though a situation in a calm, confident and positive way. Staff were also asked to use a gentle but directive approach and to make choices on her behalf on the basis of what they knew about her likes and dislikes.

### Advice regarding staffing level, programme and autism-specific strategies

It was recommended that Alice had one-to-one staff support from a small core team of staff to whom she responded well.

Staff were advised to implement a tightly structured programme to provide a predictable daily and weekly routine. A visual timetable with photos and cue cards with words was devised and used as an additional prompting strategy, and to prepare her for transitions and changes.

Alice's new programme was based on keeping her active, stimulated and happy by incorporating her interests and activities she had previously enjoyed. Staff were advised to think creatively about overcoming obstacles which had prevented Alice from being active and being outdoors in nature. One example was creative use of her mobility fund for transport.

Advice was given to make Alice's living environment more structured, quieter and less 'busy' in terms of the clutter, people coming and going, and noise levels.

The Shah 4 Stage Implementation Model was recommended with particular emphasis on monitoring progress, regular reviews and being vigilant about any signs of deterioration.

## Outcome

Initially when the above was implemented properly Alice responded very well and recovered from the catatonia-related difficulties and started enjoying a varied programme of activities and was happier. However, due to complex service-related issues, it became difficult for staff to implement the psycho-ecological approach. This led to Alice developing catatonia-type movement difficulties again, albeit at a much milder level than before. In a new placement, the catatonia management guidelines have been invaluable to staff and Alice is recovering from the catatonia and enjoying a good quality of life.

# Chloe
## Background

Chloe featured in Chapter 3. She is a young person with a diagnosis of Asperger syndrome who has shown symptoms of catatonia from the age of eight years. Her manifestations of catatonia have been described in detail in Chapter 3. Chloe's needs related to mild catatonia were understood and managed well by professionals in the children's services. However, when she had the most severe manifestations of the catatonia while studying for A levels, her difficulties and the seriousness of her catatonic episodes were not understood or appreciated by professionals in the adult mental health services. Chloe was referred to me to provide advice on treatment, management and care for severe episodes of catatonia and her overall mental health needs.

## Application of the psycho-ecological approach
### Assessment

Detailed assessment was carried out and information collated from the following sources:

- A psychological assessment of Chloe based on psychometric assessment, self-report questionnaires, observations and interviews was completed.

- An interview and discussions with Chloe's mother and staff at the autism day service which Chloe attended since her breakdown were carried out. The ACE-S and sections of the DISCO were used as semi-structured interview questionnaires.

- A perusal of relevant documents was undertaken. These included early diagnostic reports, school reports, current day-service reports and notes written by both Chloe and her parents describing the onset of catatonia and details of episodes of catatonia. The medical history and current medication was also noted.

### Diagnosis and formulation

In addition to the high functioning autism, Chloe had a tendency to develop mental health breakdown which could be shown by any of the following:

- catatonia – varied manifestations since childhood; severe catatonia deterioration during A levels which continued to worsen

- increase in complex rituals, compulsions and fixations

- fluctuating levels of arousal leading to shutdown or impulsive behaviour.

The formulation was complex and based on an understanding of Chloe's complex autism and personality, cognitive profile and factors which caused her to become overwhelmed, stressed, anxious and over-aroused.

From childhood, Chloe had shown a marked tendency to react disproportionately to sensory stimuli, emotional arousal and anything she perceived as negative. She could become overwhelmed by sensory or emotional overload. She had a tendency to react in two extreme ways. She could become hyper-aroused, excitable and act in an impulsive way or develop inappropriate obsessions. At the other extreme, she could become stuck in rituals or go into shutdown and catatonic states.

Chloe's high intelligence, awareness of her difficulties and a desire to achieve and function as a neuro-typical person were a constant battle for her. She had cumulative failure experiences. She felt strong emotions but was not able to express these appropriately and a build-up of the emotions and frustrations led to breakdown in various ways as described above.

## Strategies based on the psycho-ecological approach

- Chloe was highly sensitive to psychiatric medication. The first strategy was to review Chloe's psychiatric medication and make a plan to withdraw the anti-psychotic and antidepressant medication she was on. The family was able to work on this with the local medical professionals, and fortunately, Chloe did not suffer severe withdrawal effects.

- Psycho-education was provided in the form of a detailed report and explanation about catatonia, management and the formulation with regard to Chloe's vulnerability to the different types of breakdown. This was supplemented by a training session with staff at the autism centre which Chloe attended.

- A crisis management plan was drawn up to prevent Chloe being treated medically or in hospital during a catatonic episode unless there was a medical emergency. A community-based team was involved to provide support at home in case of crisis.

- Advice was given to the autism service based on Chloe's cognitive profile, interests and needs for novelty, sensation and stimulation.

- Besides the general prompting and support strategies, specific strategies were used to prevent movement difficulties and freezing episodes. These included one-to-one support at the start of each day for planning the structure for the day and the use of alarms and personal reminders on her phone as external prompts to move on to the next activity. Cognitive refocusing strategies of involving Chloe on neutral practical activities rather than verbal conversation were also useful.

- The local clinical psychologist and the specialist autism counsellor were able to support Chloe and the family and implement psychological components of the psycho-ecological approach. Mindfulness and cognitive refocus and cognitive restructuring strategies were incorporated to enable Chloe to self-regulate and to reduce the escalation of anxiety, arousal and repetitive thoughts. Over time, Chloe learnt to recognise early signs of anxiety and could avoid escalation and non-coping by being mindful and taking herself out of potentially overwhelming situations. She also learned to use cognitive refocusing strategies successfully.

## Outcome

Chloe and her family found the psycho-ecological approach invaluable in a number of ways. The detailed diagnosis and formulation were important for improving professionals' understanding and acceptance of the catatonia, and getting constructive professional support and services. Chloe, her family, the staff and local professionals were able to implement different components of the psycho-ecological approach. The multi-dimensional strategies enabled Chloe to improve gradually and the frequency and severity of her catatonia decreased gradually. Currently, she experiences slowness and short freezing episodes at times but these are manageable and do not escalate or impact on her daily functioning. For a few years now, she has not had any long episodes of freezing, shutdown or severe catatonia which had previously impacted on her wellbeing, independence, achievement and lifestyle. She is finally able to follow her dream of going to college, and hopefully will get her ambition and life back on track with renewed insight, optimism and hope.

# Zoe
## Background
Zoe's story was discussed in Chapter 4. It is included here to illustrate the application of the psychological components of the psycho-ecological approach in autistic individuals with very high intelligence.

Zoe did not have a diagnosis of autism when she had a breakdown after leaving university. She had masked her difficulties in social situations by using elaborate rules and strategies which she had worked out intellectually and by observation of relationships in films. Zoe experienced various manifestations of catatonia including the following:

- episodes of freezing for long periods (up to eight hours)
- difficulty initiating movement and actions
- partial and complete mutism
- movement abnormalities including waxy flexibility.

Zoe also experienced eating difficulties at times and occasional 'paralysis' of breathing and had the feeling that her muscles had frozen.

Zoe suffered devastating secondary effects and consequences of the catatonia and breakdown. These included significant loss of independence on daily living activities, becoming housebound, and withdrawing from college and an inability to work.

## Application of the psycho-ecological approach
The game changer for Zoe's life was getting a diagnosis of autism and catatonia. In Zoe's case, the most important components of the psycho-ecological approach were analysis of the possible causal stress factors

relating to her individual profile of autism and empowering Zoe to use this self-knowledge to develop coping strategies and self-management.

The stress factors related to key aspects of Zoe's autism profile included the following:

- demands in novel or unexpected social situations when she could not survive by her 'masking' strategies

- becoming overwhelmed sensorially (due to her autistic tendency to be drawn to perceptual and visual details)

- the demands of being in a romantic relationship and not knowing intuitively how to behave or cope

- the need to navigate life and every social situation in a cognitive and intellectual way with reasoned explanation and justifications rather than being able to go with the flow with intuition and spontaneity, which was exhausting for Zoe and stressful when the cognitive logic did not work

- putting great pressure on herself to understand everything with an existentialist perspective

- difficulty in maintaining an occupation to match her high intellectual ability and her need for cognitive and mental stimulation.

## Outcome

The diagnosis of autism and catatonia, the psychological formulation of her underlying autism profile and stress factors, and recommendations empowered Zoe to validate her difficulties, to understand herself better and to adjust her expectations and goals for herself. Within three months of the diagnosis and consultation, Zoe wrote us a thank you letter which spoke volumes about the outcome. The relevant extract is copied below:

> I wanted to thank everyone at the centre for everything you have done for me this year. I went through a devastating few years of confusion and serious mental illness in the lead up to the diagnosis, but the understanding and kindness of all those involved in my assessment has given me the chance to move forward with confidence and hope.

Since my assessment, I have been volunteering at a charity shop and managing my catatonia and autism well to the extent that I have not had any noticeable freezing episodes. The expertise, care and attention to my diagnosis have completely lifted my mental health issues and delusional attacks of self-misunderstanding. I occasionally 'slow down' when in overload – for which my threshold has increased remarkably since my mental health has improved – but I can still move. I can recover quickly and completely independently with anxiety management and problem-solving. This has given me the confidence to look for work, and I have secured two interviews for academic library positions which is what I now hope will become my main career. Once I have some employment security and long-term confidence in my wellbeing in place, I'm hoping to find a way into autism advocacy and/or catatonia research in thanks for the help that was the final piece in the puzzle to bring me back to life.

Zoe did in fact secure the job at an academic library. Her progress and self-management has continued as she has noted in a follow-up email:

I feel very nearly 'recovered' from my catatonic breakdown and capable of managing autism well enough to prevent a relapse, as it were. I have occasional shutdowns, but I have plenty of warning and can forestall their onset for as long as I need to before I find a safe, quiet space to shut down and reset. I always remain mobile. My executive functioning is gradually returning to the level it was at prior to my breakdown, and I'm also no longer on my medication.

Zoe's courage, insight and determination to help herself to recover and make progress is truly admirable and will be inspirational to many other people. By giving permission to include her story here, Zoe has already started helping others gain insights, hope and courage.

## Jay

Jay's life and story were described in Chapter 4 on misdiagnosis and misconception. To recap, Jay was a high functioning autistic man who was articulate and independent and who enjoyed various interests including travelling independently on public transport in London. Jay's catatonia and breakdown was misdiagnosed and he was treated with a variety of anti-psychotic, antidepressant and anti-epileptic medications. The consequences of misinterpreting his difficulties have been discussed in Chapter 4. The section on Jay's difficulties relating to catatonia and breakdown described in Chapter 4 is copied below for easy reference.

> By the time of my assessment, Jay's catatonia and breakdown had deteriorated to the point where he was unable to get out of bed or a chair, or carry out any voluntary movements or actions without prompts or assistance. Jay also showed a whole range of posture and movement abnormalities. These included stooped posture, stiff movements, dystonia, rocking, body jerks and twitching, grimacing, facial contortions and involuntary smiling, teeth grinding, continuous blinking and repetitive mouth movements. Jay also had difficulty holding his head up or looking up. His whole demeanour was lifeless (apart from the uncontrollable repetitive movements). There was no joy or spark in him. Every little action was a huge effort for him, and there was no way he could communicate his struggle, his imprisonment and his sorrow. The secondary effects included incontinence, loss of skills and independence, an inability to pursue his special interests and a very poor quality of life. Jay was also unable to continue his part-time voluntary office job at a special school. It was distressing and of great concern to his family to witness the gradual and severe deterioration and the negative effects of the psychiatric medications. Fortunately for Jay, they took steps to obtain specialist assessment and advice before it was too late.

## Implementation of the psycho-ecological approach

- A detailed psychological assessment and formulation was carried out according to the assessment protocol described in Chapter 7. This included an assessment of Jay's underlying pattern of autism, cognitive and comprehension abilities, manifestations of catatonia, and the ecological factors in Jay's residential placement and day-care.

- The diagnostic formulation included a detailed description of the manifestations of Jay's catatonia and breakdown, and his needs in view of his breakdown and his underlying autism profile.

- Formulation about the possible cumulative effects of various causal factors contributing to Jay's continued deterioration of catatonia and breakdown was used to make detailed recommendations based on the psycho-ecological approach. These factors included the following:

- Misdiagnosis and misinterpretation of Jay's behaviour and difficulties.

- Treatment with psychiatric medication – Jay was showing various observable side effects such as the movement abnormalities and repetitive movements described above. Jay may have been feeling other side effects such as increased anxiety and agitation, which he would not have been able to communicate but these may have contributed to his 'behaviour difficulties'.

- Decrease in activities, outings and interests due to being excluded when he was not ready on time or slow to respond.

- Inability to cope in day-care which was unstructured, noisy, chaotic and crowded.

- Not having the level of prompting and support he needed to initiate movement and activity.

- Not having the level of stimulation he needed in view of his cognitive and comprehension ability.

The management and implementation plan included the following elements of the psycho-ecological approach:

- Psycho-education and training based on a detailed report and additional information were used with all concerned in order to help them understand the diagnosis of catatonia for Jay, and the need for urgent review of the intervention and care plan to stop further deterioration and increase in the severity of the catatonia The reasons for Jay's slowness in responding, freezing episodes, inactivity, incontinence, and so on were explained. Strategies for the management of specific difficulties such as incontinence and episodes of agitation were implemented. Misconceptions about Jay being stubborn, lazy and uncooperative were dispelled.

- Staff training was aimed at understanding catatonia generally, and how this affected Jay. An explanation of the actual level of his cognitive and comprehension ability was helpful as staff had underestimated this. Role-play methods were used for staff to understand and feel comfortable about supporting, prompting and helping Jay with initiating movements and action. Strategies for enabling Jay to participate in outings and outdoor activities were implemented.

- Psychiatric medication was gradually withdrawn as Jay's diagnosis of catatonia and breakdown was accepted.

- Jay needed to be in a smaller, quieter place with much higher levels of structure, routine, predictability, stimulation, activity and staffing (with one-to-one support initially). It would have been impossible to achieve this in his current day-care placement. A case was made for Jay's care plan to be reviewed with a view to Jay attending a small, specialist day centre for autistic adults, and for funding to be made available for one-to-one support for Jay for a few months to implement the recommendations and to kick-start Jay's recovery and stop further deterioration of the catatonia.

## Outcome

Jay made rapid improvements in various aspects when the above plan was implemented and his difficulties were conceptualised, understood and treated differently. Jay's posture, movement abnormalities, fluidity of movements and activity levels improved remarkably quickly. His demeanour changed to relaxed, happy and content and there was no trace of the torment and anguish seen previously. He was no longer stooped; he could hold his head up and his posture was relaxed. His movements improved to the extent that he started walking well and was able to sprint, and was able to keep up with his peers. Jay still needed prompts to get started on daily routines, but he responded faster and also could carry out various routines himself, such as dressing himself. He started enjoying activities and outings and helped with household chores.

Jay started attending a small day centre which was specialist for autistic adults. The manager and staff at the centre developed a special interest in catatonia and requested psycho-education, training and psychological advice for Jay. This enabled them to support Jay and rekindle his engagement in interests and activities. They made use of the various strategies of the psycho-ecological approach and adapted them for Jay as necessary. Jay made significant progress and has been able to overcome a lot of the debilitating aspects of catatonia. He has been able to carry out a whole range of activities with enthusiasm and interest. His current programme (11 years since the assessment) is varied, beneficial and stimulating. It includes physical activities (e.g. cycling), work and home skills training, table-top and learning activities and outings and special interest project work. The latter has enabled Jay to rekindle his special interests including reading maps and timetables, travelling on public transport and enjoying outings in London.

Jay still has remnants of the catatonia and the breakdown which he suffered. He remains passive and needs prompts to get started, and others to organise him and his programme. There is not much improvement in his speech, but he does communicate by writing his responses to simple requests and choices. However, he is now free from the debilitating effects of the catatonia and the downward spiral of increasing shutdown, immobility and inactivity which could have consumed him. He is stress free, relaxed, happy and content and enjoying his life, once again exploring the sights of London by public transport and engaging in varied activities which are meaningful for him. His is a story of great sorrow and sadness with many regrets but a happy ending!

## Shaan

Shaan's story with regard to developing a complex pattern of catatonia and breakdown complicated by the side effects of various psychiatric medications over the years has been described in Chapter 4. After the diagnosis of catatonia and breakdown, and a comprehensive psychological and ecological assessment, I had made detailed recommendations based on the psycho-ecological approach. The specialist autism placement was unable to change their ethos and could not implement the changes recommended. Shaan continued to deteriorate and was transferred to another residential service for autistic adults with complex needs. The staff in the new service found it challenging to understand Shaan's catatonia and complex presentation and needs, and found it difficult to know how to start engaging Shaan in any activity. My recommendations looked good on paper but what was the point if they could not be implemented? Shaan's parents and I were beginning to despair, and I wondered if this was perhaps not the right approach for Shaan. At his parents' insistence, the service availed of further training from me to understand Shaan's catatonia and breakdown and to discuss ways they could implement the recommendations in my report. Their interest in catatonia and commitment to improving Shaan's life was uplifting, but I still left with confused feelings of hope and worry for Shaan. I wondered whether they would be able to move forward with the recommendations and how Shaan would respond. I also wondered with great trepidation whether anyone would believe that Shaan's psychiatric medications were not helping him and take the risk of gradual withdrawal.

I continued to hear from Shaan's parents but there was not much progress, and there remained huge difficulties with the recommended plan which was agreeable and acceptable to all but impossible to implement consistently. The final update from Shaan's parents in response to my request for permission to include Shaan's story in this book has enabled me to finish Shaan's story on a positive note!

> Shaan is now doing very well after a very difficult time. Since the autism practitioner started in January, she has overseen Shaan's clinical care and the implementations of your recommendations, and this has made a big difference, by ensuring greater consistency and autism understanding. Shaan's medication is being gradually withdrawn. It is reported to me that Shaan's processing is much quicker on most days and that he is more alert than ever. There have been very few episodes of catatonia in the last two to four months – just getting in and out of the car on occasions. There have been a reduced number of challenging behaviours compared to previously. He goes out somewhere every day. He goes for walks, to the supermarket and goes out for a pub meal every week and to his favourite burger place. As I am writing this down, the changes have been remarkable – we are so pleased with the emerging outcomes.

## Other brief applications of the psycho-ecological approach

- Many parents/carers of autistic individuals who are either not able to get a diagnosis of catatonia or while waiting for the diagnostic assessment have benefited from written information and general management guidelines made available by the author. This has enabled many individuals and parents/carers to start the immediate support strategies of prompting, positive support, cognitive refocusing and activity and stimulation therapy.

- In some cases, staff or managers of a service attending the training on autism-related catatonia has enabled them to conceptualise the individual's difficulties as being due to an onset of catatonia. This has enabled them to change their strategies and use components of the psycho-ecological as appropriate. The positive outcome of this for a particular individual was highlighted by the manager of an autism service who reported as follows:

> After attending the training, I realised that X's difficulties and apparent non-cooperation and neglecting himself on self-care aspects and spending hours in the bathroom were due to catatonia. On my return, I spoke to the staff team and implemented the strategies of verbal and physical prompts, one-to-one support and physical assistance to enable him to move on, eat properly, etc. X responded well to this and started improving within a few weeks. Activity and stimulation therapy was also implemented. X has gained the weight he has lost, he is interacting more, his sleep pattern has returned to a healthy one and he is more active. All in all his quality of life has improved.

- Some high functioning autistic individuals who have episodes of shutdown and catatonia have contacted me from the UK and various parts of the world. They have been helped by confirming the diagnosis (by paper, telephone or Skype video call assessments), writing letters of explanation and support to relevant authorities and service providers so that their difficulties and needs for support are believed and recognised. Partners, spouses or carers of some of these individuals have found it useful to adapt and apply some of the strategies discussed in the book.

# Epilogue

This book has been an attempt at describing and drawing attention to a devastating condition which can affect as many as one in six autistic individuals and play havoc with the wellbeing and lives of the individuals and their families in so many different ways. Catatonia, shutdown and breakdown can affect both autistic children and adults along the whole spectrum. It is not restricted to those with severe autism and learning (intellectual) disability but can affect those with high intellectual abilities and subtle autism. There are autistic children and adults who are unable to continue their education at school or university, or who are unable to work or live independently or achieve their potential due to catatonia and related breakdown. There are autistic individuals in residential care who are unable to enjoy any activity or quality of life. Also, there are autistic individuals who experience frightening and debilitating temporary 'paralysis' during episodes of shutdown and catatonia but function well at other times.

We can barely imagine the frustration and the torment for the autistic individual who shuts down, becomes unable to initiate action, or to move, respond, speak or act when or in the way they want to. We know that it is not apathy or a question of will as those who have been able to describe it refer to being 'unable' and 'locked in' rather than 'unwilling'. Trapped and imprisoned within their own bodies and mind, unable to complain or shout for help – surely not a state to be envied or to be taken lightly or ignored! As illustrated by the real-life stories of individuals and their families, the repercussions, consequences and secondary effects of the breakdown are equally if not more devastating both for the individual and their families.

In spite of these serious concerns and the growing awareness of the condition, it is tragic that there is still very limited recognition and constructive help and support accessible to individuals and their families.

We need a serious campaign to increase awareness that psychological distress, autistic stress, anxiety and non-coping can have huge negative impact on autistic individuals, and can lead to shutdown and catatonia-related manifestations in those vulnerable to this type of breakdown. This campaign needs to be worldwide and aimed at increasing awareness, not only in professionals in the mental health, learning disability and autism services but a lot more widely. We also need to increase awareness in schools, colleges and universities, and among health professionals such as general practitioners and neurologists, and teachers, parents, families and carers of autistic children and adults. Anyone providing mental health or learning support to autistic individuals at university or in the workplace needs to have training on these aspects so that timely and effective support can be provided with understanding. The same applies to specialist social workers, police officers and professionals in the criminal justice system so that individuals with behaviours related to shutdown and catatonia are not misunderstood or misjudged.

Professionals, carers, parents and families can start implementing the psycho-ecological strategies while waiting for official diagnosis, which may be difficult to access. Parents and teachers need to be vigilant about children and young people (particularly girls) who may mask their difficulties in social situations. Early signs of non-coping and breaking down need to be picked up before the difficulties escalate and they start shutting down and/or develop catatonia and/or breakdown. It is important to recognise the increased vulnerability in those who are in the passive subgroup.

For those in whom the catatonia is chronic and has affected their functioning and quality of life, it will be important to use the psycho-ecological approach to find pragmatic solutions and models of support, services and funding which can reduce the impact of the catatonia and improve the quality of life for the individual and their families.

At this point in time, we do not have any answers about the underlying neuro-psychological and biological mechanisms to explain catatonia and shutdown. We do not understand the mechanisms and psycho-physiological correlates of why and how stress, distress and non-coping affect the brain functioning of individuals who shut down, break down and show the varied manifestations of catatonia as described in this book. Moskowitz (2004) has suggested that general catatonia may be due to an intense evolutionary-based fear response, closely related to the tonic immobility strategy used by animals in threatening situations. There is some interesting research on ways in which stress may be related to brief shutdown and freezing in neurotypical people (Arnsten, Mazure and Sinha 2012). These researchers have suggested that under everyday stresses, the pre-frontal cortex can shut down, allowing the amygdala (responsible for regulating emotional activity) to take over, inducing mental paralysis and panic. This can affect conscious self-control and executive function. It is encouraging that research is focusing on possible neural circuits responsible for the freeze response in stressful, fear-inducing and threatening situations. This line of research will have huge implications for understanding autism and catatonia.

Research may one day elucidate the underlying neuropsychological and physiological mechanisms and brain processes and circuits involved in autism catatonia, shutdown and breakdown. It is also possible that the neuroscience underlying these conditions may remain elusive as it has for other intriguing and enigmatic aspects of autism such as uneven and unusual cognitive profiles, islets of exceptional ability and savant skills. We have to wait and see. For now, our priority has to be to harness research and clinical resources to make a positive difference to those affected by these devastating conditions, to prevent future misconception and reduce the risks for others. We cannot afford to remain in our ivory towers of ignorance and complacency any longer.

# Autism Catatonia Evaluation (ACE-S)

## Description

The Autism Catatonia Evaluation (ACE-S) has been developed by Dr Amitta Shah, consultant clinical psychologist in clinical practice. It is a framework for a systematic assessment and evaluation of catatonia manifestations in autistic children and adults. It can be used by anyone involved with an autistic individual in whom catatonia, shutdown and/or autism breakdown are suspected or as a screening tool for these aspects during other mental and physical health assessments. A version of the ACE-S can be downloaded from www.jkp.com/catalogue/9781785922497. Amitta Shah is happy for people to photocopy ACE-S as a full document and use it responsibly with acknowledgement. Please do not photocopy or circulate any part-section on its own.

## Uses

The ACE-S can be used for the following purposes:

- to guide assessment, recognition and diagnosis of catatonia, shutdown and breakdown in autistic individuals
- to describe and evaluate catatonia manifestations in autistic individuals
- to establish baselines and monitor progress
- to plan strategies, support and services and inform care plans or research purposes.

## Instructions and caution

1.  The ACE-S is not a quick diagnostic checklist for categorical assessments, and it is not suitable for quantitative evaluation. It is a dimensional framework for collecting information in a systematic way to build up an overall picture of the manifestations of catatonia, shutdown and breakdown in autistic individuals.

2.  The ACE-S is not suitable for a direct assessment of the individual at a given point in time. It cannot be used to elicit the information by interviewing the person concerned or getting them to demonstrate the catatonia manifestations. Users need to be aware that there can be a lot of variation in the amount of difficulty shown by the individual on different days and in different situations. Thus, it is essential for users to get information about the individual from a variety of sources to get a full picture.

3.  The ACE-S should be completed by using information from individuals – parents, carers and teachers, and so on – who have known the person and are able to give an overview of their functioning, deterioration and difficulties in different situations. This can be supplemented by information from direct observation of the individual in different settings, video footage and psychological assessment to build up the whole picture. Information from multi-disciplinary assessments such as speech and language therapy assessment and occupational therapy assessment can also be useful to supplement the information for particular sections.

# SECTION A - DETERIORATION
## (INDEPENDENCE, SPEECH, ACTIVITY)

*This section (together with Section B) is crucial for diagnosis.*

*Not be used as a checklist but to build up an overall picture.*

Evaluate if there is a **change** and **deterioration** in the individual compared to previous levels of functioning and independence in the following areas:

## 1. Slowness
Is the individual showing obvious and noticeable slowness in movement, speech or in responding verbally or actively to an instruction?

Previous level .................................................................

Current level .................................................................

## 2. Self-help/personal care skills
(getting up, washing, personal hygiene, continence, dressing, eating)

Previous level .................................................................

Current level .................................................................

## 3. Independence
(occupying self, going out, carrying out activities)

Previous level .................................................................

Current level .................................................................

## 4. Mobility

Previous level .................................................................

Current level .................................................................

## 5. Speech (fluency, flow and volume)

Previous level .................................................................

Current level .................................................................

## 6. Level of activity

Previous level .................................................................

Current level .................................................................

## 7. Evaluation and brainstorm box

Make notes about possible time of onset, timeline and possible psycho-ecological factors which could be causing stress, distress or non-coping.

.................................................................

.................................................................

.................................................................

.................................................................

.................................................................

.................................................................

.................................................................

.................................................................

.................................................................

.................................................................

.................................................................

.................................................................

.................................................................

.................................................................

# SECTION B – MOVEMENT DIFFICULTY AND SHUTDOWN

*This section (together with Section A) is crucial for diagnosis.*

*Not be used as a checklist but to build up an overall picture.*

Evaluate if the individual is showing any of the following. The difficulty should not be fleeting but last at least five minutes, *or* the person needs an external prompt to move on or complete the action.

## 1. Stopping/freezing mid-action

Description............................................................

Frequency.............................................................

Length of time (longest noted)..........................................


## 2. Getting stuck
(e.g. getting out of bed, chair, car or toilet seat; walking)

Description............................................................

Frequency.............................................................

Length of time (longest noted)..........................................


## 3. Getting stuck at transitions
(e.g. door thresholds, stairs, kerbs, escalator)

Description............................................................

Frequency.............................................................

Length of time (longest noted)..........................................

## 4. Eating difficulties

(taking long, difficulty with fork and knife, chewing and swallowing difficulty)

Description..................................................................

Frequency....................................................................

Length of time (longest noted).............................................


## 5. Getting stuck in postures

(unusual postures, crouching, kneeling, etc.)

Description..................................................................

Frequency....................................................................

Length of time (longest noted).............................................


## 6. Prompt dependence

(verbal or physical prompt needed to move, initiate or complete action or activity)

Description..................................................................

Frequency....................................................................

Length of time (longest noted).............................................


## 7. Shutdown

(can affect individual in different ways – e.g. withdrawing totally from the external environment, curling up in a ball, inability to move or respond to anything external, non-communicative, or only able to engage in self-initiated repetitive actions and unresponsive)

Description..................................................................

Frequency....................................................................

Length of time (longest noted).............................................

# SECTION C - MOVEMENT AND BEHAVIOUR ABNORMALITIES

*These may occur together with items in Section A and Section B but are not diagnostic of autism catatonia in themselves. They are useful to note and describe as part of the autism catatonia picture.*

## 1. Posture and movement abnormalities

(e.g. twisting of neck, head, upper torso, grimacing, uncontrolled dystonic movements, shaking, tremor, etc.)

Description..........................................................................

Frequency...........................................................................

Length of time (longest noted)................................................

## 2. Complex sequences of repetitive movements

Description..........................................................................

Frequency...........................................................................

Length of time (longest noted)................................................

## 3. Other miscellaneous movement abnormalities

Description..........................................................................

Frequency...........................................................................

Length of time (longest noted)................................................

## 4. Episodes of uncharacteristic inappropriate behaviour

(catatonic excitement)

Description..........................................................................

Frequency...........................................................................

Length of time (longest noted)................................................

# SECTION D - OVERLAPPING CATATONIA/AUTISM FEATURES

*These are characteristic features of autism which overlap with catatonic features. The presence of these features is NOT diagnostic of autism catatonia. These are useful to note and useful for the overall diagnostic picture if these occur for the first time or if there is marked deterioration in severity/frequency.*

## 1. Movements
(e.g. odd gait, odd hand postures, rocking, grimacing, mannerisms, complex repetitive movement such as spinning)

Description............................................................

Frequency............................................................

Time of onset.........................................................

## 2. Speech and vocalisation
(e.g. immediate and delayed echolalia, repetitive noises and vocalisations)

Description............................................................

Frequency............................................................

Time of onset.........................................................

# SECTION E - AUTISM BREAKDOWN

*Evaluate if the individual is showing autism breakdown in addition to the autism catatonia. This will need a qualitative judgement based on the overall picture of the following phenomena.*

## 1. Exacerbation of autism
a. Increased social withdrawal, isolation, avoidance of social situations

. . . . . . . . . . . . . . . . . . . . . . . . . . . . . . . . . . . . . . . . . . . . . . . . . . . . . . . . . . . . . . . . . . . . . . . .

b. Increased communication difficulties

. . . . . . . . . . . . . . . . . . . . . . . . . . . . . . . . . . . . . . . . . . . . . . . . . . . . . . . . . . . . . . . . . . . . . . . .

c. Increased repetitive and ritualistic behaviour

. . . . . . . . . . . . . . . . . . . . . . . . . . . . . . . . . . . . . . . . . . . . . . . . . . . . . . . . . . . . . . . . . . . . . . . .

## 2. Decrease in tolerance and resilience
(easily disturbed, irritable, angry)

. . . . . . . . . . . . . . . . . . . . . . . . . . . . . . . . . . . . . . . . . . . . . . . . . . . . . . . . . . . . . . . . . . . . . . . .

## 3. Increase in 'challenging' behaviour
(e.g. self-injurious behaviour)

. . . . . . . . . . . . . . . . . . . . . . . . . . . . . . . . . . . . . . . . . . . . . . . . . . . . . . . . . . . . . . . . . . . . . . . .

## 4. Decrease in concentration, focus

. . . . . . . . . . . . . . . . . . . . . . . . . . . . . . . . . . . . . . . . . . . . . . . . . . . . . . . . . . . . . . . . . . . . . . . .

## 5. Decrease in engagement and enjoyment

. . . . . . . . . . . . . . . . . . . . . . . . . . . . . . . . . . . . . . . . . . . . . . . . . . . . . . . . . . . . . . . . . . . . . . . .

# SECTION F – SECONDARY DIFFICULTIES

*This section is not for diagnosis. It is for evaluating the secondary effects and can be used for planning support, services and monitoring progress.*

## 1. Effects on independence

Description. . . . . . . . . . . . . . . . . . . . . . . . . . . . . . . . . . . . . . . . . . . . . . . . . . . . . . . . . . . . . . .

## 2. Effects on occupation
(school, college, job, training, activities)

Description. . . . . . . . . . . . . . . . . . . . . . . . . . . . . . . . . . . . . . . . . . . . . . . . . . . . . . . . . . . . . . .

## 3. Mobility and muscle wastage

Description. . . . . . . . . . . . . . . . . . . . . . . . . . . . . . . . . . . . . . . . . . . . . . . . . . . . . . . . . . . . . . .

## 4. Medical and physical problems
(e.g. severe weight loss, difficulty passing urine, distorted breathing)

Description. . . . . . . . . . . . . . . . . . . . . . . . . . . . . . . . . . . . . . . . . . . . . . . . . . . . . . . . . . . . . . .

## 5. Effect on quality of life

Description. . . . . . . . . . . . . . . . . . . . . . . . . . . . . . . . . . . . . . . . . . . . . . . . . . . . . . . . . . . . . . .

## 6. Effects on parents, family, carers
(e.g. stress, inability to work, go out, etc.)

Description. . . . . . . . . . . . . . . . . . . . . . . . . . . . . . . . . . . . . . . . . . . . . . . . . . . . . . . . . . . . . . .

# Further Information

This book together with the ACE-S can be used a resource for psycho-education and training. This can be either general or targeted for a particular individual based on their ACE-S profile and other assessments discussed in the book.

## Enquiries and referrals for specialist assessment, training and consultancy

Dr Amitta Shah can be contacted at the following centres:

Leading Edge Psychology
Clinical Psychology Consultancy Centre
Email: amittashah@gmail.com
Email: amittashah@onetel.com

The NAS Lorna Wing Centre for Autism
Email: lornawingcentre@nas.org.uk

# References

APA (American Psychiatric Association) (1952) *Diagnostic and Statistical Manual of Mental Disorders*, 1st edn. Washington, DC: APA Press.

APA (American Psychiatric Association) (1968) *Diagnostic and Statistical Manual of Mental Disorders*, 2nd edn. Washington, DC: APA Press.

APA (American Psychiatric Association) (1980) *Diagnostic and Statistical Manual of Mental Disorders*, 3rd edn. Washington, DC: APA Press.

APA (American Psychiatric Association) (2000) *Diagnostic and Statistical Manual of Mental Disorders*, 4th edn. Washington, DC: APA Press.

APA (American Psychiatric Association) (2013) *Diagnostic and Statistical Manual of Mental Disorders*, 5th edn. Washington, DC: APA Press.

Arnsten, A., Mazure, C. and Sinha, R. (2012) 'This is your brain in meltdown.' *Scientific American 306*, 48–53.

Baron, M., Lipsitt, L. and Goodwin, M. (2006) 'Scientific foundations for research and practice'. In M. Grace Baron, J. Groden, G. Groden and L. Lipsitt (eds) *Stress and Coping in Autism*. New York: Oxford University Press.

Billstedt, E., Gillberg, C. and Gillberg, C. (2005) 'Autism after adolescence: Population-based 13- to 22-year follow-up study of 120 individuals with autism diagnosed in childhood.' *Journal of Autism and Developmental Disorders 35*, 3, 351–60.

Bleuler, E. (1908) Die Prognose der Dementia praecox (Schizophreniegruppe). *Allgemeine Zeitschrift fur Psychiatrie und Psychisch-Gerichtliche Medizin 65*, 436–64.

Bräunig, P., Kruger, S., Shugar, G., Hoffler, J. and Borner, I. (2000) 'The catatonia rating scale I – development, reliability, and use.' *Comprehensive Psychiatry 41*, 2, 147–58.

Breen, J. and Hare, D. (2017) 'The nature and prevalence of catatonic symptoms in young people with autism.' *Journal of Intellectual Disability Research 61*, 6, 580–93.

Bush, G., Fink, M., Petrides, G., Dowling, F. and Francis, A. (1996) 'Catatonia. I. Rating scale and standardised examination.' *Acta Psychiatrica Scandinavica 93*, 129–36.

Cohen, D., Nicoulaud, L., Maturana, A., Danziger, N. *et al.* (2009) 'Investigating the use of packing therapy in adolescents with catatonia: A retrospective study.' *Clinical Neuropsychiatry: Journal of Treatment Evaluation 6*, 29–34.

Consoli, A., Gheorghiev, C., Jutard, C., Bodeau, N. *et al.* (2010) 'Lorazepam, fluoxetine and packing therapy in an adolescent with pervasive developmental disorder and catatonia.' *Journal of Physiology Paris 104*, 309–14.

Davies, J. and Read, J. (2018) 'A systematic review into the incidence, severity and duration of antidepressant withdrawal effects: Are guidelines evidence-based?' *Addictive Behaviors.* Sept 4. https://doi.org/10.1016/j.addbeh.2018.08.027.

De Sanctis, S. (1908) 'Dementia praecocissima catatonica oder katatonie des fruheren kindersalters?' *Folia Neurobiologica 2*, 9–12.

DeJong, H., Bunton, P. and Hare, D. (2014) 'A systematic review of interventions used to treat catatonic symptoms in people with autistic spectrum disorders.' *Journal of Autism and Developmental Disorders 44*, 2127–36.

Dhossche, D. (1998) 'Brief report: Catatonia in autistic disorders.' *Journal of Autism and Developmental Disorders 28*, 329–31.

Dhossche, D., Shah, A. and Wing, L. (2006a) 'Blueprints for the assessment, treatment, and future study of catatonia in autism spectrum disorders.' *International Review of Neurobiology 72*, 267–84.

Dhossche, D., Wing, L., Ohta, M. and Neumarker, K. (2006b) *Catatonia in Autism Spectrum Disorders.* San Diego, CA: Elsevier.

Fink, M. and Taylor, M. (2003) *Catatonia: A Clinician's Guide to Diagnosis and Treatment.* Cambridge: Cambridge University Press.

Fink, M., Taylor, M. and Ghaziuddin, N. (2006) 'Catatonia in autistic spectrum disorders: A medical treatment algorithm.' *International Review of Neurobiology 72*, 233–44.

Ghaziuddin, N., Dhossche, D. and Marcotte, K. (2012) 'Retrospective chart review of catatonia in child and adolescent psychiatric pationts.' *Acta Psychiatrica Scandinavica 125*, 33-38.

Ghaziuddin, N., Gih, D., Barbosa, V., Maixner, D. and Ghaziuddin, M. (2010) 'Onset of catatonia at puberty: Electroconvulsive therapy response in two autistic adolescents.' *Journal of ECT 26*, 4, 274–7.

Ghaziuddin, N., Nassiri, A. and Miles, J. (2015) 'Catatonia in Down syndrome: A treatable cause of regression.' *Neuropsychiatric Disease and Treatment 11*, 941–9.

Grandin, T. (2006) 'Stopping the Constant Stress: A Personal Account'. In M. Grace Baron, J. Groden, G. Groden and L. Lipsitt (eds) *Stress and Coping in Autism.* New York: Oxford University Press.

Groden, J., Cautela, J., Prince, S. and Berryman, J. (1994) 'The Impact of Stress and Anxiety on Individuals with Autism and Developmental Disabilities.' In E. Schopler and G. Mesibov (eds) *Behavioural Issues in Autism.* New York: Plenum Press.

Hare, D. and Malone, C. (2004) 'Catatonia and autistic spectrum disorders.' *Autism 8*, 183–95.

Hutton, J., Goode, S., Murphy, M., Le Couteur, A. and Rutter, M. (2008) 'New-onset psychiatric disorders in individuals with autism.' *Autism 12*, 373–90.

Joseph, A. (1992) 'Catatonia.' In A. Joseph and R. Young (eds) *Movement Disorders in Neurology and Neuropsychiatry.* Oxford: Blackwell.

Kahlbaum, K. (1973 [1874]) *Katatonie oder das Spannungsirresein. Eine klinische Form psychischer Krankheit.* Trans. Y. Levi and T. Pridou. Baltimore, MD: Johns Hopkins University Press.

Kakooza-Mwesige, A., Wachtel, L. and Dhossche, D. (2008) 'Catatonia in autism: Implications across the life span.' *European Child & Adolescent Psychiatry 17*, 327–35.

Kraepelin, E. (1907 [1903]) *Psychiatrie: ein Lehrbuch für Studierende und Ärzte,* 7th edn. Leipzig: J Ambrosius Barth. (Abstracted and reprinted: *Clinical Psychiatry: A Textbook for Students and Physicians.* New York: Macmillan.)

Leary, M. and Hill, D. (1996) 'Moving on: Autism and movement disturbance.' *Mental Retardation 34*, 39–53.

Leekam, A., Libby, S., Wing, L., Gould, J. and Taylor, C. (2002) 'The Diagnostic Interview for Social and Communication Disorders: Algorithms for ICD-10 childhood autism, and Wing and Gould autistic spectrum disorder.' *Journal of Child Psychology and Psychiatry 43*, 327–42.

Lishman, W. (1998) *Organic Psychiatry: The Psychological Consequences of Cerebral Disorder.* Oxford: Blackwell.

Maudsley, H. (1867) 'Insanity of Early Life.' In H. Maudsley (ed.) *The Physiology and Pathology of the Mind.* New York: Appleton.

Mazzone, L., Postorino, V., Valeri, G. and Vicari, S. (2014) 'Catatonia in patients with autism: Prevalence and management.' *CNS Drugs 28*, 3, 205–15.

Moskowitz, A. (2004) '"Scared stiff": Catatonia as an evolutionary-based fear response.' *Psychological Review 111*, 984–1002.

Nylander, L. and Gillberg, C. (2001) 'Screening for autism spectrum disorders in adult psychiatric out-patients: A preliminary report.' *Acta Psychiatrica Scandinavica 103*, 429–34.

Ohta, M., Kano, Y. and Nagai, Y. (2006) 'Catatonia in individuals with autism spectrum disorders in adolescence and early adulthood: A long-term perspective study.' *International Review of Neurobiology 72*, 41–54.

Park, C. and Park, J. (2006) 'Living with Autism: A Collaboration.' In M. Grace Baron, J. Groden, G. Groden and L. Lipsitt (eds) *Stress and Coping in Autism.* New York: Oxford University Press.

Rogers, D. (1992) *Motor Disorder in Psychiatry: Towards a Neurological Psychiatry.* Chichester: Wiley.

Sacks, O. (1982) *Awakenings* (revised edn). London: Pan Books.

Shah, A. and Wing, L. (2006) 'Psychological approaches to chronic catatonia-like deterioration in autism spectrum disorders.' *International Review of Neurobiology 72*, 246–63.

Starkstein, S., Petracca, G., Teson, A., Chemerinski, E. *et al.* (1996) 'Catatonia in depression: Prevalence, clinical correlates, and validation of a scale.' *Journal of Neurology and Neurosurgical Psychiatry 60*, 326–32.

Wachtel, L., Hermida, A. and Dhossche, D. (2010) 'Maintenance electro-convulsive therapy in autistic catatonia: A case series review.' *Progress in Neuropsychopharmocology & Biological Psychiatry 34*, 581–7.

Wing, L. and Attwood, A. (1987) 'Syndromes of Autism and Atypical Development.' In J. Cohen, A. Donnellan and R. Paul (eds) *Handbook of Autism and Pervasive Development Disorders.* New York: Winston-Wiley.

Wing, L. and Gould, J. (1979) 'Severe impairments of social interaction and associated abnormalities in children: Epidemiology and classification.' *Journal of Autism and Childhood Schizophrenia 9*, 11–29.

Wing, L., Leekam, S.R., Libby, S.J., Gould, J. and Larcombe, M. (2002) 'The diagnostic interview for social and communication disorders: Background, inter-rater reliability and clinical use.' *Journal of Child Psychology and Psychiatry 43*, 307–25.

Wing, L. and Potter, D. (2002) 'The epidemiology of autistic spectrum disorders: Is the prevalence rising?' *Mental Retardation and Developmental Disabilities Research Review 8*, 151–61.

Wing, L. and Shah, A. (2000) 'Catatonia in autistic spectrum disorders.' *British Journal of Psychiatry 176*, 357–62.

Wing, L. and Shah, A. (2006) 'A systematic examination of catatonia-like clinical pictures in autism spectrum disorders.' *International Review of Neurobiology 72*, 21–39.

World Health Organization (1992) *The ICD-10 Classification of Mental and Behavioural Disorders. Clinical Descriptions and Diagnostic Guidelines.* Geneva: World Health Organisation.

World Health Organization (2018) *The ICD-11 International Classification of Mental and Behavioural Disorders.* Accessed on 21/01/2019 at: https://www.who.int/classifications/icd/en

Worley, G., Crissman, B., Cadogen, E., Milleson, C. *et al.* (2015) 'Down syndrome disintegrative disorder: New-onset autistic regression, dementia, and insomnia in older children and adolescents with Down syndrome.' *Journal of Child Neurology 30,* 9, 1147–52.

Zaw, F. (2006) 'ECT and the youth: Catatonia in context.' *International Review of Neurobiology 72,* 208–31.

Zaw, F., Bates, G., Murali, V. and Bentham, P. (1999) 'Catatonia, autism and ECT.' *Development Medicine and Child Neurology 41,* 843–5.